LOVEBOUND

RECOVERING FROM
AN ALCOHOLIC FAMILY

OTHER BOOKS BY PHYLLIS HOBE

Living Boldly
Never Alone
When Love Isn't Easy

LOVEBOUND

RECOVERING FROM
AN ALCOHOLIC FAMILY

by
Phyllis Hobe

NAL BOOKS

NAL BOOKS
Published by the Penguin Group
Penguin Books USA Inc., 375 Hudson Street,
New York, New York 10014, U.S.A.
Penguin Books Ltd, 27 Wrights Lane,
London W8 5TZ, England
Penguin Books Australia Ltd, Ringwood,
Victoria, Australia
Penguin Books Canada Ltd, 2801 John Street,
Markham, Ontario, Canada L3R 1B4
Penguin Books (N.Z.) Ltd, 182–190 Wairau Road,
Auckland 10, New Zealand

Penguin Books Ltd, Registered Offices:
Harmondsworth, Middlesex, England

First published by Dutton, an imprint of Penguin Books USA Inc.
Published simultaneously in Canada

First Printing, April, 1990
10 9 8 7 6 5 4 3 2

ACKNOWLEDGMENT

Excerpt from *Emmanuel's Book* by Pat Rodegast and Judith Stanton.
Copyright © 1985 by Pat Rodegast. Reprinted by permission of Bantam
Books, a division of Bantam Doubleday Dell Publishing Group, Inc.

LIBRARY OF CONGRESS CATALOGING IN PUBLICATION DATA

Hobe, Phyllis.
    Lovebound : recovering from an alcoholic family /
by Phyllis Hobe.
      p.   cm.
    Includes bibliographical references.
    ISBN 0-453-00723-6
    1. Adult children of alcoholics—United States. I. Title.
HV5132.H62   1990
362.29′23′0973—dc20   89-13370
                                             CIP

REGISTERED TRADEMARK—MARCA REGISTRADA

Printed in the United States of America
Set in Century Schoolbook
Designed by Julian Hamer

*To the adult and the child
in each of us*

ACKNOWLEDGMENTS

WRITING THIS BOOK has been a special kind of discovery for me. For one thing, it led me to a better understanding of myself because I had to go back into some parts of my past I wanted to avoid. But that was an unexpectedly rewarding experience. Among the episodes I really didn't want to live again were some valuable moments I'm glad I was able to retrieve. I had forgotten they were there, and now I have them again.

I also made the acquaintance of some exceptional men and women who are doing great things with their lives, in spite of many obstacles. I have always been an admirer of heroines and heroes, but I thought they lived in days gone by. Now I know better. The many adult children of alcoholics who shared their stories with me live in the here and now, and they live with quiet valor. They are very loving people, and to me, in today's world, that in itself is quite heroic. I wish I could name them, but we agreed that I wouldn't. They aren't looking for praise, but I hope they know they have my deep respect.

I spent many hours talking to therapists and counselors, both in private practice and in recovery programs, and I am touched by their devotion to those who come to them for help. They put more than hours into their work; they put in part of themselves. I have had the benefit of Dr. Geraldine DePaula's skill and compassion in my own therapy, and her generosity in helping me to explain how the principles that helped me might help others. I am also grateful to Karen Shulte, M.S.W., Vincent DiPascuale, Kathleen Diak, Dr. Paul Fink, Loretta Sandy, Mary Hoffman, Dr. Yvonne Kaye, Dr. Jean Kirkpatrick, Ann Smith, and Dr. Stephen Barrett for giving of their time, their experience, and their conclusions. Obviously, they care.

CONTENTS

All things in life
are dedicated to the purpose
of expanding awareness.
One never discards a portion of oneself.
One merely transforms it into Light
until the entire being is Light.

This is a minutely slow process.
You may feel as though
you are standing in the same place
as you were a month ago,
and yet you are not.
You have a month more
of life experience, and therefore
you are more aware
than you have ever been.

I say this to erase discouragement.
I do not say it to obliterate effort.
The more conscious the striving
the more rapid the growth.

—Emmanuel

PREFACE

THE FIRST TIME I heard someone use the term *ACOA*, I had to ask her what it meant. Then I learned that it meant me, an adult child of an alcoholic. I have at least 28 to 30 million brothers and sisters in the United States alone—and probably many more who don't feel free to admit it, to themselves or anyone else. It's very hard to call your mother or your father—and possibly both—a drunk.

I had known about Alcoholics Anonymous since I was in high school, when I tried to persuade my mother to attend one of their meetings and she refused. "Is *that* what you think I am?" she demanded angrily. "One of those *drunks?*" Typical of the alcoholic, she couldn't admit that she had a problem. "You just hate me because I know how to have a good time and you don't!" she told me. She was sober when she said it. Later, after a few drinks, she stood unsteadily in the doorway to my room. "You're the one who makes me drink, you know that?" she said. "I have a daughter who hates me!" Peculiarly, there was a half-smile on her face that I thought I imagined. I know now that I didn't. There were a lot of other things I didn't imagine, either, but I was absolutely incapable of believing my own eyes and ears, and even my own mind. I saw, heard, and thought what I was told to see, hear, and think, and the telling was not always given in words, but in far more subtle, intimidating forms of communication.

[1]

In those days there wasn't an Al-Anon or an Alateen, and since I wasn't an alcoholic I didn't think of going to AA for help—unless I could bring my mother with me. She was the one I wanted to rescue. I didn't know then that my stepfather also was an alcoholic. I believed him when he said he drank to keep my mother company, and I assumed that if I could rescue her, I would solve his problem as well. Many years later I was able to realize that drinking was a powerful bond between them, one I could never break. But when I was a child it was very confusing to have my stepfather agree with me (although never in my mother's presence) that my mother drank too much—and then see him fill up her glass with a flourish.

I loved my mother very much, but I couldn't tell anyone why I was worried about her. I would have felt disloyal talking about my mother's problems to her doctor or any of her friends, and besides, she would have denied them. Finally, when I was in college and really desperate, I went to a therapist—to find out what I could do to save my mother from destroying herself. It took more than a year for that therapist to awaken me to the realization that the only person I could save was myself. Now, after many more years, a great many mistakes and a few more therapists, I'm glad I did.

I welcome the amount of attention being focused on the damage that alcoholics do to their families. When I read a book or an article about adult children of alcoholics, I know I wasn't imagining what happened to me. And, unless you're one of us, you have no idea what a relief it is to say, as a matter of simple fact, that my parents were alcoholics and not feel that the sky is going to fall in on me.

As I became aware that the label ACOA was being used to describe so many people, I began to be curious about some of the things we could do to recover from the effects of growing up in an alcoholic family. I thought they might be helpful to me: I also was seeking my own kind. If there were so many men and women with experiences similar to mine, it seemed like a good idea for me to get in touch with some of them.

So I went to self-help groups and looked into recovery programs. I also talked to adults who had spent their childhood with alcoholic parents and were trying to get over the nightmarish effects of it. And I came to the following conclusions:

- If you're an ACOA and want treatment for your problems, treatment is available, no matter where you live, how serious your problems are, and how much, if anything, you can afford to pay. Recovery programs are becoming a big business. You can choose from among self-help groups, groups led by a professional counselor or therapist, inpatient programs, outpatient programs, and individual therapy. The costs vary from nothing to very high, and at least part of the fees are covered by many health insurance policies.
- A lot of people from several different backgrounds are trying to help ACOAs counteract the effects of growing up in an alcoholic family, yet most of the recovery programs are remarkably alike. Most are based on The Twelve Steps of Alcoholics Anonymous, although often the Steps are rewritten to fit in with somewhat different philosophies.
- ACOAs aren't getting the kind of help they really need because most forms of treatment tend to reinforce their problems.

When we finally get up enough courage to go into a recovery program, we already feel worthless, guilty, and peculiarly unemotional. We certainly don't experience relief after being told how many things are wrong with us—and that there isn't any cure. We grew up believing that we were to blame for our parents' drinking; when recovery programs call us "codependent" and "enabling," they add to our burden of guilt. We have always felt powerless to do anything about the condition of our lives; in recovery we are told that this is true—and it's not going to change. Instead of teaching us the skills of self-sufficiency, which we desperately need, we are urged to expect a "Higher Power" to look after us. We're afraid of our feelings and find it difficult to express them, especially our anger; in recovery we're told to "detach" ourselves from the behavior of our alcoholic parents— meaning that if the parent falls down drunk, we should be able to go about our business. And, above all, we are told, "Don't dump on our parents—they did the best they could." Most of us know that isn't true, because no matter how sick our alcoholic parents were, they could have sought help, and didn't. As children we were denied love, and now we need it more than anything else in the world; nowhere in The Twelve Steps is the word "love" even mentioned. Even the basic language of recovery is strangely lacking in emotion: words such as "dysfunctional," "codependent," "enabling," "detachment," seem more descriptive of mechanical processes than human behavior.

The literature about ACOAs falls into two categories: a technical description of the ACOA predicament and personal stories of recovery. The technical books and articles offer long lists of ACOA "symptoms" and describe our "disease" as if they were spelling out our doom, but the only prescription offered is to join a support group and practice some form of AA's Twelve Steps. The autobiographical stories, while courageously admitting the agony an alcoholic can inflict on a family, arrive at some questionable solutions to the suffering: the alcoholic parent stops drinking, usually with the help of Alcoholics Anonymous, and the ACOA goes into an Al-Anon recovery program for the rest of his life.

Alcoholic parents and their children are not reconciled simply because the parent stops drinking. A sober alcoholic may still behave like an alcoholic, and it is much more common for the alienation between parent and child to continue throughout the life of the parent and even beyond. This is something that the adult child of an alcoholic must be encouraged to confront if he or she is ever going to break free of the past.

Martin, a thirty-eight-year-old father, occasionally considers how he will feel if his own father should die. "He hasn't had a drink since I was eighteen, and that's twenty years ago, but nothing else about him has changed. He still makes life miserable for my mother, and I made sure that my children don't even know him. My brother asks me how I'll feel about that when my father dies, and I tell him, 'I'll be relieved.' " But Martin knows that he may also feel guilty about his relief because he has not yet come to terms with his conflicting feelings of love and hate toward his father.

Telling an adult child of an alcoholic parent that he must spend the rest of his life recovering from the damages of the past makes it almost impossible for him to develop a healthy self-esteem. At first he may rejoice in being able to share his experiences with others who have gone through similar ordeals, but eventually he needs to know that he can achieve an independent, productive life beyond counseling, recovery programs, and support groups. Very few treatment programs regard recovery as something that has an end as well as a beginning.

While it is encouraging to see so many programs for

recovery made available to ACOAs, I think something important has been left out of them. There is too much emphasis on the negatives in an ACOA personality and not nearly enough on turning them into positives. And even our positives are described in such a negative manner that we begin to wonder if there is *anything* right in our lives.

One day recently I came across a flyer advertising a new therapy center for ACOAs. I picked it off a stack of them on the counter of a bakery that specializes in the kind of whole-grain black bread I like. As soon as I unfolded it, I read:

Common Characteristics of Adult Children of Alcoholics

EITHER SUPERRESPONSIBLE OR IRRESPONSIBLE	HAS DIFFICULTY WITH INTIMACY
TAKES SELF VERY SERIOUSLY	HUNGERS FOR APPROVAL AND AFFIRMATION
HAS DIFFICULTY HAVING FUN	
IS VERY SELF-CRITICAL	HAS DIFFICULTY COMPLETING ASSIGNMENTS
IS FEARFUL OF LOSING CONTROL	TENDS TO LIE
GUESSES AT WHAT IS NORMAL	IS IMPULSIVE
FEELS DIFFERENT	IS EXTREMELY LOYAL

While these descriptions are more abbreviated than most, they are typically dismal. They also describe behavior that almost every human being exhibits to some degree at some time or another, whether or not there has been an alcoholic in the family. In fact, the ACOA who attends the usual recovery-program introductory lecture about the nature of his condition may leave feeling much worse than when he walked in. For instance, the word *workaholic* is almost always used to describe the ACOA who achieves, and that belittles the achievement. Many of us are in caregiving jobs and professions, yet that is often mentioned as if it were a sorry fact, as if we were trying to make ourselves, rather than someone else, feel better. It is true that we often go to extremes in taking on responsibility, and we can be sacrificially loyal, yet there is something worthwhile at the heart of these traits and that deserves some acknowledgment.

Granted, we ACOAs are a tough audience because we don't want to hear about our problems, and perhaps that is why the people who want to help us often overstate them. But not all of us lie all of the time. Not all of us are incapable of having fun. Not all of us have to live in fear of becoming addicted. Many of us bungle our attempts at relationships, but not much more than do most other people. We are said to feel empty and unfulfilled, but that is a condition common to many people who have no association with alcoholism. Most of our problems are typical of human beings in today's world—except that some of them are more intense because we don't have a lot of healthy childhood experiences to balance them.

Unfortunately, because that intensity is seldom made clear, the person who learns he is an ACOA is likely to think that everything about him is a symptom of a terrible, all-consuming ailment. In fact, some recovery program administrators like to mention that many people don't even realize they are ACOAs until someone describes the symptoms to them. "Then almost everybody sort of gasps and says, 'Hey, that sounds like me!' " one administrator told me. And when you look at the laundry list of so-called ACOA characteristics, you can understand why almost anyone would identify with many of them. In fact, if it weren't for the negative way in which those characteristics are presented, many of them would describe the kind of man or woman most people would like to be.

As for the self-help programs I have visited—and AA's is of course the most influential—there is no doubt in my mind that they are a good place for a troubled ACOA to begin seeking recovery. But I also see them reinforcing the feelings of dependency and guilt that are so much a part of our problems. Perhaps this is why many ACOAs seem to be so depressed even after years in such programs.

Rachel is a veteran self-help group member. She is forty-two but looks ten years older and twenty years more tired. During most meetings she says very little, even when the others try to draw her out. Only once did I hear her open up, and then every other sentence was punctuated with guilt for the anger she felt toward the alcoholics in her past. She began by explaining that she was the oldest of seven children born one right after the other "because my mother and father were too drunk to practice any kind of birth control. Besides, they had me to bring up their kids while they were off sitting in some bar. Then, when they came home, they'd always find something I didn't do right.

"But hell," she interrupted herself, slumping down in her chair and crossing her legs tightly, "the truth is, I'm a co-dependent, so the fault is as much mine as theirs. Anyway, alcoholism is a disease and I have to accept that." The rest of the group nodded in agreement.

"I'm much better now," Rachel went on. "I refuse to be anybody's slave now. I mean, no more double shifts at work. After I've put in twelve hours, I've done enough. That's when I tell my boss I'm going home." *Twelve hours!* That's what Rachel calls a normal day, and she still feels she has to explain why it isn't longer.

Rachel's willingness to assume responsibility for the sins of her parents is typical of the ACOA. Yet Rachel is not a beginner. She attends self-help group meetings four nights a week—in several different communities—and has been doing that for three years. She also sees a therapist once a week. She thinks she is getting better because she can see "what I did wrong" in allowing alcoholic parents to distort her life. The trouble is, she doesn't seem to know what to do right. Neither do the other members of her group. In fact, change is something they rarely discuss. They spend more time confirming each other's feeling of helplessness.

Speaking to ACOAs who have gone beyond the self-help programs is another experience entirely. Most of them speak well of their early participation in a group, but they agree that they had to look elsewhere for the self-esteem they needed to repair their damaged lives. "I found that I wasn't comfortable with anyone except another ACOA," Rusty told me, "and I knew that wasn't good for me. I needed to find out what a normal life was like."

Some women ACOAs fault the Al-Anon self-help groups for insensitivity to their special problems. And here I have to agree with them. I know personally the guilt all women feel when we can't make someone we love happy—and to be called an enabler to the abusive alcoholic parent is a load too heavy to bear, much less throw off. Very few recovery programs divide their groups according to gender; in fact, some program administrators expressed surprise when I asked whether there were separate groups for men and for women. This lack of awareness that women's needs are different may have roots in the history of AA itself. While AA was the first and, for a long time, the only organization to recognize alcoholism as a serious social, medical, and spiritual problem, it considered it to be a man's problem. Unfortunately that attitude persists, but in more subtle forms of expression. While women are clearly welcome in recovery programs today, very few programs create an environment that makes women feel understood.

Perhaps I was fortunate in having to wrestle with the problems of being an ACOA before I ever heard of the term. Or before I read the literature or attended any of the programs. In therapy, and in my sometimes awkward attempts to put my life in order, I began to see myself as an individual who could change, instead of a type imprisoned by a rigid pattern of behavior. That may be why I was surprised by the sense of helplessness I found among some of the groups I attended. At first the descriptions of an ACOA depressed me, too. Then I got mad—because I didn't feel the way I was being told most ACOAs feel. I was not living in fear of becoming an alcoholic or embracing some other form of addiction. I enjoyed close relationships, but I didn't feel trapped in them. I didn't question everything I said because it might be a lie. I didn't self-destruct or put off starting something because I might give it up. I had uncovered plenty of emotional handicaps, but I had already dealt with many of them and knew I didn't have to live with them forever. Unfortunately I was not finding that kind of a hopeful attitude—even among many ACOAs who had been in and out of one program or another over several years. Recovering from the effects of an alcoholic parent or parents may take a long time, but somewhere along the way we ought to begin to feel that we are getting somewhere.

I bristle when one ACOA reminds another not to dump on our alcoholic parents or see ourselves as victims. We did not choose our parents, and, as children, there was nothing we could do to escape their influence on our lives. We *are* victims, and the only way we can grow beyond that condition is to face up to the anger it justifiably arouses in us. There is no way we can deeply and honestly forgive what was done to us unless we allow ourselves to feel the pain we have borne and then realize, most joyfully, that we have survived it. Only when we become aware of our strengths and know that an alcoholic parent can never again hurt us, does forgiveness become possible—and even essential to our own recovery. Telling the ACOA to share the responsibility for her own wounds is like telling her to feel guilty because they hurt—and that's exactly what her alcoholic parent told her a long time ago.

The treatment programs take a different approach. They encourage ACOAs to get in touch with their emotions, but they do it in an unemotional way. "An ACOA is a very fragile person," a counselor told me, "so we have to go very slowly. It's best to start with an educational approach. We try to make them aware that they do have feelings, but we don't want to stir those feelings up." The reason for this is that many ACOAs are afraid of their emotions; they've held them back for so long that they expect something terrible to happen if they let them go. Some have such a tight control over them that they're convinced they don't have any feelings at all. But while the methods used in the treatment programs are intended to spare ACOAs any further pain, they may actually be prolonging it by postponing or avoiding contact on an emotional level. As one therapist explained to me, "Once an ACOA becomes aware that she has feelings, the next step is to learn how to express them. But if that next step isn't taken, or if it's skipped, then recovery isn't possible because the ACOA goes right on denying how she really feels. She can acknowledge that she has feelings, but she doesn't know what to do with them."

Looking back at the beginning of my own road to recovery, I can see how important it was for me to figure out what had happened to make me the way I was. But it was equally important for me to know that I felt something in response to everything that happened. Even if I couldn't identify what I felt at the time something happened, even if I blocked it out of my conscious mind because I wasn't able to deal with it, I was strengthened by the assurance of therapists that I *did* feel something—and that, with effort, I could experience it again. It struck a blow at my deepest, most incapacitating fear, which was that I couldn't feel *anything*. Realizing that I could recover those lost emotions was like discovering that half of me was missing, but could be found. That possibility helped me to get through the difficult early stages of recovery when I so often wanted to run the other way.

I disagree with the gloomy, alarmist concern about the future of adult children of alcoholics. I believe we can do something to change our lives, and many have already done a lot.

In this book I am writing as one ACOA to another about some of the things we feel and can't always express until we come to know much more about ourselves. I think that the most important thing you can do is to learn how to respect yourself as a human being with an identity of your own—and how to love the child in you who was never truly loved all the time you were growing up. That will take some time and a lot of help, but at some point along the way you will begin to feel that the two of you—your adult and your child—can handle just about anything that comes along. This ability to understand, to love, and appreciate the self is what self-esteem is all about.

Some of the experiences I describe here are mine and many are those of others who have grown up in alcoholic families and are committed to recovering from them. This book is not intended to replace any form of treatment or recovery, but will, I hope, encourage you to get the kind of help you need and perhaps keep you company along the way.

CHAPTER ONE

MEET AN ACOA

WHEN I WAS GROWING UP, we didn't use the word *alcoholic* to describe anyone we knew. Alcoholics were whiskery men and blowsy women on Skid Row, wherever that was.

Once I actually got to see a Skid Row. I was about eight, I think, and I remember riding in the backseat of a sedan, squeezed between my mother and another woman. My stepfather sat up front next to the driver, who was the other woman's husband. It was a winter evening, dark and cold, and we had to drive through the Bowery on New York's Lower East Side to get to where we were going. I could make out a few figures slouching in doorways. Some were lying on the cold, hard sidewalk. I had never seen anything like that.

"Who are they?" I asked my mother and, before she could answer, my stepfather spoke from up front. "Winos," he said.

"Poor souls," my mother said, putting her arm around me and pulling me closer. "They don't have any home to go to."

"Why not?" I asked, leaning forward to look out the window again.

"They drank it all away," my mother explained. "That's all they do, is drink." She shook her head sadly. She made it sound so voluntary. I wondered why anybody would ever do such a thing as give up a home and a family just to drink. I put my head against

my mother's shoulder and snuggled into her. I was
turning away from something I didn't want to know:
My mother and my stepfather, and the couple with
them, were alcoholics. Within a few hours, after stopping off at the home of some people they hardly knew,
they would be very, very drunk. The two men would
argue over who was going to drive home, when it
really didn't matter because both of them were haz-
ardously unfit to handle a car. The two women would
make fun of them at first, but later would assault
them verbally from the backseat all the way home.
And I, stashed between them, would struggle against
a rage that was far too enormous for a child to con-
tain. It would get the better of me, and when it did,
when I screamed something like "*Stop* it!" as the bick-
ering grew nasty, or if I started to cry, I knew what
would happen. They would turn on me, all of them,
and in the darkness of their uncontrolled, angry bodies
squirming around me, it would all be my fault. They
were only having a good time, and I was spoiling it by
reacting with fear. They would convince me that I was
wrong to feel the way I did—which didn't take much
effort because I was convinced already.

No, I did not call my parents alcoholics in those
days, nor did I even realize that they were. Alcoholics
were people like the ones we saw lying on the sidewalk or in dark doorways. My parents went to work
every day. They had good jobs and their bosses thought
highly of them. During the week we ate dinner at
home every night and went to bed at a reasonable
hour. Our neighbors were respectful. We dressed well.
We didn't have a car, but in the aftermath of the
depression very few people did. Every summer we
went away for a two-week vacation. My grades were
good and my teachers liked me. I had friends.

Yet for all the trappings of a normal family, my
parents were no different from the Skid Row bundles

they pitied. They put their next drink ahead of everything else in their lives: their home, their jobs, the
good meals, the decent clothes, each other, even their
child. They just never had to do it in a way that was
obvious to anyone but insiders—and we looked the
other way.

Family Portrait

My parents drank a lot, but during their younger
years they never drank on weekdays, except for Friday nights. That's when they began drinking, almost
as a ritual, and they did not stop—ever—until very
late Sunday night or early Monday morning. Or until
they passed out, which happened often.

I have been told that my mother drank heavily as a
teenager. My father, as far as I know, did not. My
stepfather, who married my mother when I was four,
was a serious athlete in his youth; he didn't drink or
smoke. But he came from an alcoholic family and
when he began dating my mother he wanted to keep
up with her. He started by drinking, and eventually
he began to smoke, too, because my mother suggested
that it might cure him of biting his fingernails.

All my parents' friends were drinking buddies. And
the friendships didn't last long. I remember so many
angry outbursts and vicious accusations. But always
there were new friends to replace the lost ones. Friends
are easy to pick up in bars, and bars were where my
parents spent their weekends. They used to take me
with them because it was cheaper than hiring a baby-
sitter, and that left more money for drinks. I think
they also didn't want a baby-sitter to find out about
their drinking habits. But that wasn't what they told
me when I asked them why I couldn't stay home,

which I really would have preferred. They said they loved me so much that they wanted me with them. That made me feel very guilty about wishing I could be somewhere else. I was always the only child in the bar, and that was uncomfortable. I would sit in a booth, reading a book or doing my homework, hoping I wouldn't accidently be seen by anyone who knew my friends. I would have been shocked if the parents of one of my friends walked in, because I didn't think anyone else's parents drank, but that never happened.

My parents sat at the bar. They liked to get chummy with the bartender, until sooner or later he or someone else would say something they didn't like and they would move on to another bar. We usually stayed until the bar closed, and sometimes my parents would invite the dispossessed customers to come home with us, where the drinking would continue until everyone was physically incapable of downing any more.

To me, in those years, Sunday was the longest, most agonizing day of the week. I longed for Mondays because they brought with them the guarantee that the world—or at least my part of it—had to return to sanity.

My parents had some close calls. As long as they had to use public transportation, they were spared some harm. But when they began to prosper and could afford to buy a car, they were involved in a few accidents. They managed to get out with only bruises, but one car was totaled. Sometimes they were stopped by the police for drunken driving, but someone always knew someone who could make a citation disappear. They had other mishaps they couldn't account for, such as the time my mother fell and cut her chin on a doorsill, and the time she fell again and dislocated a disk in her spine. Once my stepfather passed out with a lighted cigarette between his fingers and it burned through to the bones. (He switched to smoking a pipe after that.) Once my mother threw a potful of hot coffee in his face as he was choking her. But they never missed a day's work because of their drinking. In fact, they never were late.

Eventually, their health suffered. My mother's pretty face was twisted by an attack of Bell's palsy, and her liver was so damaged that her doctor wept. She was in and out of discreet, expensive rehabilitation centers, where she would dutifully attend all the counseling sessions and the craft classes until the day she was released. Then my stepfather would take her out for a drink because, as he said, "She sure needed one." She continued drinking—and getting drunk—even after she lost a leg to cancer at the age of seventy, and when she died of emphysema five years later, she was still smoking, or trying to, between body-wrenching attacks of coughing.

My stepfather can barely walk, but he refuses to see a doctor because he blames doctors for my mother's death. Five years ago he collapsed and spent three weeks in the hospital, hallucinating and strapped to his bed. He still drinks, but only beer, which he insists is harmless.

The Alcoholic's Child

I can describe my parents as alcoholics now and feel no guilt. In fact, it helps, because the word tells me I wasn't imagining what went on in our family. It really happened, not only to me, but to so many other people that finally somebody put a label on it. It's like finding out there's something really wrong with you so that you stop thinking you're making it up.

Now there's a label for me, too: I am an adult child of alcoholics, an ACOA. There are approximately 28 million of us in the United States alone—probably more, because one of our characteristics is that we try to deny there was ever anything wrong with our parents. Yet we were shaped by their alcoholic way of life as surely as if our genes compelled us to behave as we do. No, I am not claiming that alcoholism is an hereditary disease, or that children of alcoholics will also become alcoholics. I am not convinced that alcoholism is a disease in the sense that diabetes is, or that it is passed on genetically, and much more research will have to be done to persuade me that it is. But I do accept the results of studies that tell us that the experience of growing up in an alcoholic's home conditions a person to react to life in certain telltale ways. I think that for most of us it's a relief to find out that there is a reason for the way we are, and that we aren't alone.

We know now that life for an ACOA is such a serious business that it's hard for us to let go and have fun. We may start a lot of things, but we often give up on them too easily—yet we stick by some things and some people much too long for our own good. We don't always tell the truth, although we don't think of ourselves as liars. Actually we're covering up, not so much for our own behavior, but for someone else's. We blame ourselves for just about anything that isn't right with our immediate world, and we feel it is our job to make the people we love happy, even if they don't want to be. We try to please all of the people all of the time, and when we don't, we think we didn't try hard enough.

Obviously we carry a lot of guilt around with us. We want people to approve of us, but we don't want them to get close to us because we think they won't like what they see—which makes friendships hard to come by. We constantly feel endangered, so it's important for us to be in control of our lives—and everyone else's. Any change is threatening to our sense of security. We take risks easily, which some people consider admirable. Don't be fooled by it—we just don't know how to look out for ourselves. We've lived on the brink for so long that we don't realize how disastrous one more step might be. We think other people are okay—and we're not. We want instant gratification; we don't believe in promises because too many have been made and broken. But we'll also give you something for nothing because we don't think we deserve anything in return. We think we have to work harder and do better than anybody else in order to be good enough, or else we figure, "What's the use of trying!" and we don't.

Granted, these are characteristics that most people, not only ACOAs, will recognize as some of the ordinary negatives any human being picks up along the way. The difference is that in an ACOA they are more intense and painful because there has been very little else in their lives. They can't count their blessings, because they don't have any. What was normal for them would be considered bizarre by most other people. Yet they don't look for sympathy because they don't think they need any. The ACOA's problem is that he or she doesn't feel entitled to anything. We're the kind of people who don't yell "Ouch!" when we bump into chairs. Instead, we apologize to them.

Love Is a Double Bind

So—now that we have a label and a list of identifying marks, what do we do with our lives? We go back into our past and look for the missing half of ourselves. We put together the childhood we never had, and we begin to build a future that is right for us.

Many ACOAs are discovering that, while our past will always be with us, we can actually repair some of the damage that was done there. We can give ourselves the nurturing that everyone needs and we didn't get. And, no matter how late we begin, we can look forward to a life that is worthwhile and fulfilling. A life that has relationships, self-confidence, hope, endurance, accomplishment, emotional freedom, honesty, trust, openness, spontaneity, self-sufficiency, and enjoyment. Above all, a life with genuine love in it, and that is something an ACOA has never had. In fact, the greatest obstacle to our recovery is that we don't know what real love is when we see it.

To an ACOA, love is a double bind. It's what keeps us tied to the alcoholic/s in our lives, yet it's the only thing that can set us free. I realize that this will take some explaining.

In the life of an alcoholic, there is no such thing as love. There is only the word; it is used often and it is used diabolically to manipulate, to enslave, to confuse, and even to destroy anyone who can be of use to the alcoholic in his or her pursuit of a drink. *But there is no love.* There are broken promises, abuse, neglect, deceit, disappointments, blame, humiliation, and pain beyond credibility—and the alcoholic calls it love. It's the way he treats himself, as well as everybody else. Now, if you're a child with a normal human need to love and be loved, and if you grow up in an alcoholic family where you're constantly being told that what you're getting is love and not pain, you're going to believe it. There is nothing in your experience so far to contradict it.

No, you won't be satisfied with what you're getting. Something inside of you will sense that it isn't what love ought to be. But since you're blamed for everything anyway, you'll automatically blame yourself for wanting something you don't have. Or for wanting something different. You will look at yourself through the eyes of the alcoholic and you'll tell yourself that you're greedy, demanding, selfish, ungrateful, and, worst of all, not lovable. You'll rationalize that if you're not getting the love you want, it's because you haven't done enough to earn it. You'll accept the fault as yours, never the alcoholic's. So you try harder to give the alcoholic what he or she wants, and you may actually be grateful for the pain you get in return—because you've been conditioned to believe that it's love.

Later, in your attempts at other loving relationships, when you get hurt by someone else who claims to love you—and you'll be drawn to such people—you won't object. By then you'll believe that pain is part of love, maybe even the proof of it. You won't even allow yourself to *feel* the hurt, because the accusations you would heap on yourself would be more than you could bear.

I can remember explaining to a high school girlfriend that the reason my mother was so embarrassingly drunk was that I was born when she was very young and she had sacrificed her whole life for me. As you can imagine, I had heard those words many times before, but I was beginning to believe they were mine. I can also remember wondering if my second husband was right when he accused me of ruining our marriage because I was hurt by his infidelities. Another ACOA I know blamed his obesity as a child for the fact that his alcoholic father used to beat him. To this day he says, "I think, in his own way, he loved me."

Children know better. They can sense when they're loved and when they aren't. But at that early stage in life, their instincts and observations need confirmation. One voice, one person saying, "Yes, you're right, this isn't the way people love each other," might make a difference, but in an alcoholic family that isn't likely to happen. Even a parent who doesn't drink is so caught up in a pattern of denial that he or she will assure the child that the alcoholic parent really loves him. Under that kind of pressure, children find it safer to forget the truth as they know it.

Why, then, doesn't an ACOA look for the right kind of love somewhere else?

We do. We look everywhere and we try everything. But it's almost impossible to recognize something we've never seen. Real love, if we should stumble across it, scares us. It doesn't feel right because there's no pain. We don't trust it. We keep thinking that there is nothing wrong with love as we know it—we just need the "right" person to give it to us. And of course the "right" person usually is someone who appears to be very different from the alcoholic in our lives—and turns out to be exactly the same. Gender has nothing to do with it: I married two men, and almost married a third, who were like my mother. As my therapist commented when I came to that realization, "At least you can't say there was no progress—you went from worst, to worse, to bad instead of the other way around."

You the Parent and You the Child

The only way for an ACOA to begin to recover from an alcoholic family is to experience genuine love from the inside out. We have to learn how to love ourselves in the true sense of the word before we can undo the damage done by the pain we were given in love's place. And ironically, we who have never known love are the only ones who can teach ourselves what it is.

Freeing ourselves from our alcoholic families is a long, difficult procedure—and worth every bit of the effort. It means we have to be willing to change—not overnight, but radically—into a very different kind of person than we have been. In a sense, it's like starting our lives again, except that this time we have to become our own parent.

There are three things an ACOA has to learn: how to be an adult, how to be a child, and how *not* to mix them up. The child in each of us is still there, yet it has never known a childhood. It has never experienced silliness, wonder, easy laughter, inquisitiveness, or spontaneous anger. It has never known comfort for a hurt, protection from what it fears, encouragement for what it wants to attempt, or appreciation for what it is. It has never known the satisfaction of bringing pleasure to someone simply because it exists. It has never found joy in its own being. Similarly, the adult in each of us has always been there, but was never developed. It wasn't available to give the child what it needed to be a child. Instead the child responded to its alcoholic parents by trying to take on adult responsibilities—an impossible feat. The result was failure— and the pain of knowing it.

Coaxing this unchildlike child out of the dark corner of ourselves where it thinks it belongs will not be easy. And only one person can do it: the adult that each of us is capable of becoming, the adult whose growth was stunted by living with parents who were incapable of giving us lessons in maturity. The adult still has the potential to grow strong enough and wise enough to meet not only our present needs, but those of the child so long neglected. There is, within each of us, the possibility for a new parent-child relationship that is healthy, regenerative, productive, and free of ghosts. In a sense, we can start over and set things straight: the child being a child, and the adult looking after both of them. Once this happens, the ACOA is released from the past, from the endless attempt to get the love we need from someone who is incapable of giving it to us.

But—that's not the end of the story. Because this is not a fairy tale. After being released from bondage, the ACOA has to learn how to live in the real world.

We have to learn what a relationship means; what to give to it and what we want to get from it. We have to learn how to draw the line between our own needs and those of someone else. We have to stop looking for someone to take care of us—and trust ourselves to do it. We have to give up trying to make things happen, or to stop them from happening; we have to give ourselves a chance to face up to whatever comes along. We have to allow ourselves to make mistakes—and maybe learn something from them. We have to forgive us this day our trespasses and try to forgive those who have trespassed against us. We have to do something with our anger; we can't just let it sit there. And what are we going to do with all our love?—with all the love that nobody wanted and we still have to give?

Recovering from an alcoholic family may take the rest of your life—but it will be a better life. You will need a lot of help, but there is a lot of it out there if you know where to look. And eventually, when you feel ready, you can help someone else. That's something you'll want to do, because, believe me, it's part of the recovery.

CHAPTER TWO

FINDING A LOST CHILD

SARA WAS THE OLDEST of four children, and she learned to drive as soon as the law allowed. "We all did," she says, "because almost every night one of us had to go out and retrieve my father."

Dinnertime was important in Sara's family. "My mother always wanted us together at the dinner table, and I can remember when it used to be my favorite time of day. My father drank then, but not as much. He had a great sense of humor and could always make us laugh. And we'd all talk about what we did during the day. If we had something on our mind, we'd talk about it. My father never got nasty when he drank. He just fell asleep in his chair.

"But later he began to drink more, or maybe he just couldn't handle it, and we'd start calling around to find out where he was because my mother wanted him home for dinner. Usually he'd be at the Elks or the VFW, and by then he'd had a lot to drink and one of us would go and get him."

Sara remembers one night in particular. She was seventeen and starting her first year in college. "My brother Randy was going to be sixteen in a few days, and I was looking forward to him getting his license so I wouldn't always be the one to pick up my father."

It was a fall evening and Sara drove slowly because it had rained that afternoon and there were wet leaves in the streets. She found a parking space in front of the Elks Club building and squeezed into it just as her father came out. He was with a few other people and Sara hoped he wouldn't bring them over to the car. She didn't like these friends of her father. Oh, maybe they weren't so bad, but they were like all the others, loud and raucous, and she was uncomfortable when they got close to her. She couldn't stand the smell of their breath and the way they climbed all over her. She sat very still in the darkness until they passed and stopped at the car parked behind her.

"Then, all of a sudden, they drove off and I didn't see my father. I thought he must have gone along with them. 'You sonofabitch!' I remember muttering. 'You *knew* I was coming to get you!'

"I put the car in reverse and I was so mad I was going to gun the engine, but then I decided that wasn't a good idea. I remembered there were those wet leaves in the street and I didn't want to skid, so I opened the door and looked back to see how much space I had. And I saw my father lying on the wet ground! It's a wonder I saw him at all because he was wearing a black raincoat, and it was dark outside. I could just see his head and his chest, with the left rear wheel aimed at his gut. If I had backed up I would have killed him!

"I never even thought of getting help, yet all I had to do was walk into the Elks and somebody would have been there. But no, that wasn't the way we did things in our family. We weren't going to let anybody know about my father. We lied for him, made excuses for him, covered up for him. Dumb! People knew. Don't you think everybody in the Elks knew he was drunk that night? For God's sake, they were right there in the same room with him. But no, we never admitted that. All we ever thought about was, *Don't let anybody find out that he's drunk!*

"I got out of the car and I could see he was unconscious. I was afraid he might have hit his head when he fell. I started pulling at him, trying to lift him up high enough to put him in the backseat. I'm a pretty small person, but somehow I managed to do it. I was crying so hard I could barely see the road as I drove home. Halfway there my father came to, and guess what he said to me? He said, 'Hey, what d'ya think about little Randy getting his driver's license?' As if nothing had happened.

"I exploded. I started screaming, 'I don't give a damn about Randy getting his fucking license! Why should I give a damn about that? I almost killed you, damn you!' I felt terrible talking to him like that, but he was so drunk I don't think he heard me. I can't explain how I felt—I hated him and I loved him at the same time."

Sara still finds it painful to remember that night. Even at seventeen she liked to think she was an adult, but in some off-limits part of herself, she knew it wasn't true. She was a child trying to handle an adult-sized problem and doing a very poor job of it. She had been doing that all her life.

What the Label Means

The term *adult child* can be misleading because it seems to describe an adult who is still partly a child. But that isn't an accurate description. *Adult child* is someone who has been masquerading all his life, first as a child and then as an adult. He doesn't really know how to be either one.

In his early years he imitated other children because he was small and had to fit in with them, but he never allowed himself to feel like a child because it wasn't safe. To be a child, you need to live in a secure environment where you can express your emotions freely. In order to explore your world and find your own strengths and limitations, you need protection from danger and guidance through difficulty. To gain confidence in your ability to take care of yourself, you need someone telling you, "Go ahead—try! I'll be here if anything happens."

A child who grows up in an alcoholic family has none of these assurances. He is punished for expressing emotions that make the parent uncomfortable, and the touchy points can vary from day to day. He has no protection from harm and is almost constantly exposed to the danger of a parent's unexpected hostility. He will never be encouraged to step out on his own because that would sever his bondage to the alcoholic parent.

The child of an alcoholic parent goes through the motions of being a child and comforts himself with the promise that when he grows up he will live the way he chooses. But that doesn't happen, because unless we have the security, protection, and affirmation that a child requires, we don't become adults. We can only pretend that we do. And the ACOA begins pretending very early.

Becoming Aware of the Child

I grew up convinced that I was a perfectly functioning adult because I had so much experience looking after my parents. I thought I was especially mature because I went to a therapist for help with problems I couldn't handle. And as soon as the immediate problem was solved, or appeared to be, I thanked the therapist and went on my way. If anything, I thought I was too adult because I couldn't just let go and have a good time—but there were worse things in life, I told myself.

As the phrase goes, "when I least expected it," I was overwhelmed by a complete upheaval in my life. My second marriage was in trouble, my relationship with my parents was agonizing, and the coauthor of a book I had written was suing me to recover all rights to it. Since I hadn't been in therapy for several years and had moved during that time, I asked a psychiatrist friend where to go for help. She referred me to Dr. Geraldine DePaula, a Philadelphia psychiatrist, who introduced me to the concept that in each person there is a child and an adult. It was the single most important thing I have learned in my life.

I was in a wretched emotional state when I first talked to Dr. DePaula. My immediate concern was the threat of a lawsuit because, obviously, I had to respond to it in some way. I had never been sued, never been involved with lawyers (except for my first divorce, which was almost an automatic procedure). I had been told I would have to go to New York, where the suit had been filed, to make a deposition, and I didn't even know what that meant. I had engaged an attorney, but I was struggling to pay his fees. My husband had left and come back and was still not sure he wanted to stay. But he was thoroughly opposed to my desire to defend myself and my work, and I was torn between his disapproval and my conviction that I had to protect my work. My mother had just elected to have her left leg amputated and refused to get a second opinion before the surgery.

Recently, when I asked Dr. DePaula to explain the concept of the relationship of the adult and the child in each of us, she recalled some of our early conversations.

"When you had to go to New York to make a deposition, you anticipated the trip with total dread. It was a miserable experience for you. You felt overwhelmed, intimidated, abused, taken advantage of—everything about it was negative.

"So I asked myself, *Why is this woman having such a hard time? I know that she's capable. I know that she knows what went on in her work with her coauthor. I know that she can present this story to me. Why can't she present this story to the attorneys?*

"Then, as you were describing how you felt, it was almost as if, right before my eyes, you turned into a very scared little kid who was overwhelmed by the legal process. A great deal of a person's poor self-esteem comes from the child, who feels unloved, unappreciated, inadequate, inept—all the things that little children are made to feel when they're not functioning as full adults (and it's totally absurd that they *should* be expected to do that). But at that point the relationship between the adult and the child is such an unconscious one that the person doesn't even realize a child is involved. She just thinks it's the way she is—which doesn't feel very good.

"When I realized this was going on in you, I knew that the first thing I had to do was address it—and the second thing was to make *you* aware of it. You actually had to become conscious of the fact that there *were* two separate parts of yourself instead of seeing them as one. Until you could do that, sometimes you'd feel like a shaky adult and sometimes like a shaky child, but you'd never be sure who was in charge of what—and you wouldn't be able to call on one or the other, consciously, to handle certain situations. You needed to separate the two instead of seeing them as one person, so that you could assign each of them appropriate responsibilities. For instance, there were certain things that the adult part of you needed to do to protect the child from the legal process you were involved in. Making a deposition was a job far beyond the capacity of a child to do. But it was appropriate for an adult to do it. At the same time the adult had to protect the child from that level of responsibility—because the child simply couldn't handle it.

"There are age-appropriate tasks for people to do. I mean, you wouldn't want to put a five-year-old child on a witness stand and ask her how she wrote a book, would you? Or how she worked with a coauthor? If you think about actually doing such a thing, it becomes ludicrous! On the other hand, the adult—who actually worked with the coauthor and had actually written the book—well, *she* could be on the witness stand. And *she* could make a deposition and be perfectly reasonable about what she presented.

"Once you began to be aware of the difference between the adult and the child in you, we were able to talk objectively about the adversarial nature of the legal process. Your adult could understand that it was the opposing attorney's task to try to throw you off kilter—you could even appreciate the sort of sadistic game involved in the process. And you could prepare to meet that challenge."

I remembered doing that. Dr. DePaula pointed out that my own attorney would also be present at the deposition, and it would be his job to protect my legal rights during the questioning by the opposing attorney. She explained that all I needed to do was tell what happened—"Just the facts, ma'am," as Joe Friday might have said. I didn't have to offer opinions or anything else—only the truth as I recalled it. Above all, she said, leave my emotions out of it.

Can you guess what happened? As I began to look at the situation from the point of view of my adult, I actually began to feel better about it. I thought I had a fighting chance. I had an excellent memory—most writers do. I could also remember details in sequence and could relate them coherently—again, thanks to my writer's training. When necessary, I could choose my words carefully and remember exactly what I had said and how I said it. If my adversary attempted to bully me, which I suspected might happen, then my best defense would be simple, concise answers. Hey, I wasn't in such bad shape, was I?

"But, you see, if the child goes in to handle such things, then it becomes an agony, a torture, for the person every time," Dr. DePaula said.

Once I began functioning as an adult, I began to sense the child part of me in a very different way. Being separated from my adult made my child become more real to me. Dr. DePaula and I even began referring to her as Little Phyllis and my adult as Big Phyllis. We imagined how I would take Little Phyllis with me on the trip to New York, making sure that I brought along a few of her dolls and storybooks. But when we arrived at my attorney's office, Little Phyllis would stay in the reception room while I went inside for the deposition proceedings.

"We had to imagine it that way," Dr. DePaula explained, "in order to make the split between the child and the adult so conscious that if you started to feel like a terrorized child in there with the attorneys, you could say, 'Wait a minute! I know I left Little Phyllis out there in the waiting room with her dolls and storybooks. *She's* all right.' That would enable you to go back to being your adult again in a very conscious way. Then, just as consciously, you could go on sitting there in the hot seat, but knowing the child was okay in the other room."

This is something I still do. And probably always will. There are times when I'm caught off guard. Something can trigger a response that makes the child rush in just as she always used to do. But now I'm conscious of it. I can call the child back with a, "Hey, honey, it's okay. You stay here—I'll take care of this."

I can't say that I breezed through the deposition, or the long legal wrangling that went on for almost two years after that. But I did pretty well. What's more important is that ten minutes into the proceedings, I began to feel okay about myself. I could actually see that a game was going on, and with each volley of questions and answers I felt more sure of myself. It felt good to be an adult. And it felt good to know my child was out of harm's way. Occasionally I would imagine her, curled up in one of the vinyl-covered green chairs in the reception room, turning the pages of the book she loved to read—and that image gave me a reassuring sense of inner serenity.

As Dr. DePaula explained, separating the child from the adult within ourselves makes it possible for the adult to understand and meet the needs of the child. "The adult begins to think in terms of normal child development," she said. "For instance, what are normal things that children are capable of? And what kind of protection do children need to enable them to grow? I mean *grow* in every sense of the word—not only grow physically, but grow emotionally, grow in responsibility, grow in being able to understand things. The adult is the one who can help the child do these things.

"Sometimes it helps people to become aware of the two parts of themselves if they work with a transitional object first. I'll often send clients out to buy a teddy bear or a stuffed rabbit. And not just any old teddy bear or rabbit or whatever. It has to be chosen with care. Then, if they let themselves go on sort of an automatic pilot, they begin to realize that the person who really picked out the bear or the rabbit was the child. And that it was the adult who had the generosity to allow the child to do the picking. This is one of the ways we begin to distinguish between the needs of our child and the capabilities of our adult. We begin to understand that children need to be protected, and that there are certain things adults shouldn't ask little children to do because it's inappropriate."

Our Missing Childhood

Children of alcoholics are the nicest kids you'd ever want to meet. Everybody wants to take them home. They're very well behaved, they do as they're told, they don't talk back, they never get bratty, and they're completely devoted to their family, especially their parents. They're easy to spot because there's something special about them—most people call it "maturity"—that's unusual at such a young age. As Mary Hoffman, coordinator of treatment at Caron Family Services, explains, "ACOAs are more mature at six than you and I are at twenty-one—because they have to be the parent to their parents. They take on too much responsibility for a child to handle, so they really don't have a childhood."

That's the way Sara was as a child. From a very early age she could see that her mother (who was not an alcoholic) had all she could do to look after her father. So Sara took on the mothering of her younger sister and two brothers—and her mother and father as well. She helped change diapers, clean the house, cook the meals, and do the laundry. She didn't have to be asked to baby-sit, and although she loathed giving up her free time, she never complained. She didn't mind the work. "It was that constant feeling of trying to keep something awful from happening that got to me," she recalls. She learned arithmetic as she sat beside her mother, watching her struggle to pay the family bills with very little money. "I was always aware that money was scarce," she says. "Somehow my mother managed to see that we got what we needed, but there was never enough for extras. My father didn't make much money, and he was good at getting other people to buy him drinks, but what he spent on drinking hurt the rest of us."

Sara didn't know how to have a good time. She still doesn't, but she's trying to learn. "My father's idea of giving us a good time was to take us down to the VFW on Sunday afternoon and buy us each a Coke. We knew he only did it so he could have an excuse to drink, and we'd sit there nursing our Cokes and watching him get drunk. But he'd tell us to smile and have fun, so we'd smile and make him think we were having fun. God, how we hated it!

"Now, when I'm with people who are drinking, I get very uptight. I watch them closely to see if they're getting drunk, and the moment they start slurring or laughing too loud, I'm out of there. My husband says he can tell how I feel from across the room—it's as if someone put a broomstick up my back."

When I was a child, I used to feel as if I had to become a different person when I was with other children my age. First of all, I didn't want them to know about the problems in my family. But I was very burdened by those problems, which made me feel old when I was with other children. I thought there was something wrong with that, so I used to watch my friends and classmates very closely and imitate their behavior. If my parents could have seen me, they wouldn't have recognized me! I could laugh, even giggle, and become almost carefree, but none of it was real. Playing house, when I was very young, was a strange experience. I couldn't do what the other children did, which was to mimic what went on in their own homes. So I'd offer to play the child, which I didn't do any too well, until I caught on to how my friends played their parents. Then I'd mimic my friends mimicking their parents.

I had some dolls, but I never played with them. I took good care of them and made them pretty clothes, but to me there was something sad about them. Unresponsive. My favorite toys were stuffed animals. They were soft and cuddly, like the real animals I loved so much but couldn't have because we lived in apartments where animals weren't permitted. It always seemed to me that animals offered such consistent expressions of love. They never licked you one minute and bit you the next.

Becoming Our Parent's Parent

When we ACOAs were children, we tried to act like adults because somebody had to—and our parents wouldn't. If only one parent was an alcoholic, the other was so busy looking after him that there was no time for anyone else. We were the kids who always said, "No, I can't," when other kids were going off for a good time. We had more important things to do: go home and take care of our parents. We had to be there to distract them from drinking or to persuade them not to be violent or to make them happy so they wouldn't want a drink. When none of our efforts worked—and sooner or later, they didn't—we blamed ourselves for letting our parents down.

Even before I was old enough to go to school my mother often talked to me as if I were the adult and she were the child. She confided in me about everything—her fears, her resentments, her disappointments, her friends, her marriage, her job, her health, and her dread of death. I remember listening to her intently, taking in every word and understanding nothing. Yet inside me I felt a terrible urgency to say something that would make her feel better, because she seemed to expect me to find solutions to her problems. "Your life is so much better than mine was at your age," she used to say wistfully, and I took that to mean that I was born owing her something. So I tried to get out from under the debt by searching my inexperienced soul for some scraps of the wisdom she insisted I had. It was a futile effort; my problem-solving cupboard was bare. Yet those "adult" conversations were the only times when I was able to get close to my mother, and I was afraid that if I didn't give her what she needed, she would look elsewhere —in short, that she would leave me. Frantic, I did what every child excels in doing: I "read" my mother. If she wanted me to be the parent, then I would do it. I watched her expression, her mood; I noted the change in her voice and the twitching of her foot as she crossed one leg over the other. How often did she reach for a cigarette? How far down did she smoke it before she crushed it out? If she was melancholy, I became a clown to make her laugh. If she was tired, I persuaded her to rest. If she was angry at a friend she thought had betrayed her, I gave her my devotion. If she complained that her boss didn't appreciate her, I told her she was wonderful. When she married my stepfather and they argued, I looked upon myself as their peacemaker.

I tried to give my mother everything she thought she didn't have. I tried to make myself indispensable to her because, in my child's mind, that was the only way I could hold onto her and insure my own survival. I would *make* her love me!

From my present vantage point, I can look back and

see that my mother may have wanted to be a good parent, but she certainly didn't know how. And, typical of the alcoholic, she refused to admit that she could do anything to help herself. She expected other people, even her child, to take care of her. She was the only child she permitted to exist in her world.

In many ways my mother counted on me for the comfort and care a child naturally expects from a parent, which made it impossible for me to count on her for the same things. I was frightened by her dependency on me. Child though I was, I knew something about our relationship was lopsided. If she, the primary adult in my life, was unable to look after herself, what was going to happen to me?

Why Do We Do It?

People often wonder why children take on responsibility for an alcoholic parent at such an early age. Is it a lack of intelligence? A superabundance of compassion for an incompetent someone close to them? Are they blindly idealistic? Out to take over? I think the answer is far more simple: survival. A child of alcoholic parents knows instinctively—as does any other child—that its very existence depends on the care and nurturing it gets from its parents. And if the parents are incapable of giving that care, if they are so unstable that they look to the child for *their* nurturing, then the child will do whatever it can in a desperate attempt to make them strong enough to take care of the child. At that stage of life, the child has no other choice; it cannot take care of itself. In order to survive, to go on living, it makes a one-sided deal with the parents: *I will pretend to be the parent if only you will stay with me.*

Illogical, yes, but what more can you expect from a child? To say no to the parent's needs is too dangerous. The parent just might walk away and never come back, and, as any child knows, abandonment is the same as death. Bolstering the parent therefore becomes as urgent a matter as the child's own breathing.

Repeating the Pattern

Unfortunately, unless something happens to break the stranglehold the child and the alcoholic parent have on each other, we ACOAs will pursue the same self-defeating strategy in other relationships throughout our lives. We're attracted to people who want to be the child and who want us to be the parent because that's the only kind of relationship we know, and the moment we feel someone needs us, we're hooked into feeling responsible for them. Why? One reason is that we weren't able to make our alcoholic parent happy, and we feel guilty about it. So we try again with someone else, especially someone who offers us the same kind of relationship we had with our parent. It's our way of trying to gain control over the forces that control us: unconsciously we believe that if only we can succeed in making someone happy, we will gain that person's love and everything will be all right. It never is, because once again we are attempting to do the impossible. A more compelling reason for our attraction to unreasonably dependent people is that under our make-believe adult exterior we are still frantic children trying to make a parent strong enough to keep us alive. So maybe we do look a little puzzled when someone asks us why we don't let our hair down and have some fun. Fun? You have to be a child to have fun, and we never were.

We weren't the kind of kids who went racing out the door on Saturday mornings to be with our friends. We hung out at home. We didn't sleep over because we were afraid something bad would happen while we were away. We didn't want our friends to sleep over in our house because there were things we didn't want them to see.

Ask Martin why he has to work at having a good time and he'll tell you that he didn't have any practice as a child. "Not once, not one single night, did my father ever come home before eleven o'clock," he remembers. "And the minute I heard his key in the door I could tell he was drunk. So I'd always get up and try to keep him from waking my mother and my little brother. I'd sit at the kitchen table with him for hours, listening to him tell me how rotten his life was, and I'd try to talk him into going to bed. Did you ever try to talk sense to a drunk? Don't waste your time. That's what I did for years, and all I ever got for it was circles under my eyes.

"When I was a teenager I never went out with my friends. Hell, I didn't have any friends because I never wanted to go anywhere. I always wanted to be there when my father came home because I knew how nasty he could get when he was drunk, and I didn't want anything to happen to my mother and brother. In all honesty, he never hurt any of us physically, but he used to threaten to. And once—I can still see him coming down the stairs carrying my kid brother, holding a big carving knife up to his throat and telling my mother and me he was going to kill him. Somebody—maybe my mother—called the police—and they came and locked him up for a couple of days. But my mother wouldn't press charges, so they let him go and he came home.

"I couldn't go out and have fun when I knew something like that might happen. I can't do it now, either, and here I am, a grown man with a family I love. It's not that I don't like people, because I do. But when I'm out socially, I always tell people that if I don't appear to be enjoying myself, it's because I'm an accountant. I try to joke about it and make my work the scapegoat, but I know what the real reason is."

Why You Didn't Grow Up

An adult is a person who knows how to take care of herself. She doesn't have all the answers, but she's willing to look for them. She knows that her feelings are important because they're telling her what kind of a person she is and what she needs to stand on her own two feet. She looks after herself because she realizes that if she doesn't function well, she won't be able to look after anyone else. She knows what she can give to the world and what she has to get from it.

The person who grows up in an alcoholic family is exactly the opposite. She has needs, too, but no one pays attention to them and that convinces her that they are unimportant. Her alcoholic parent is the star of the family show. His or her needs are always in the spotlight, and if they aren't gratified, there is hell to pay. Eventually the child of such a parent is able to tune out the voices of her own needs to such an extent that she no longer realizes they exist. "I'm fine, thanks," she'll tell you, standing in the midst of chaos, trying to put the pieces of her family's life together. She has no sense of herself, no awareness of what she can and can't do; she can't express joy or yield to sadness because she never felt free to honor her own feelings. On the contrary, she tries to be everything to everyone, and of course she fails. She constantly makes promises she can't possibly keep, and she can't tell the difference between an expectation that is reasonable and one that is unfair. She lives to please others, never herself, so no matter what she achieves, she has no sense of satisfaction. Everything she does she brings as a gift to someone who tears open the wrappings, looks inside the box, and tosses it aside with a surly, "Oh, *that* isn't what I wanted." She goes from sour note to sour note and her life is empty, no matter how many people dwell there.

"I finished college and was holding down a good job. The only way for me to go was up—but do you think I realized that?" Fran asks. "I was living with a guy who treated me like a doormat, and I let him do it. He worked when he felt like it and he'd rather die than lift a finger to help me. He expected me to work all day and come home and cook a big meal for him. If he couldn't find a pair of clean socks, you'd think the world was coming to an end—and of course it was all my fault.

"It took me a long time to break things off with him because I kept thinking he must be right and I must be wrong. I was trying to make him happy, just the way I used to try making my father happy. I remember when I was a kid, and my father would start drinking and get mean, I'd climb up on his lap and put my arms around him and try to calm him down. I was his favorite, at least that's what everybody told me, and I thought I was the only one who could keep him from tearing the house apart. I was so scared of him that I had to steel myself to be nice to him when he was that way.

"It was the same thing with the other men in my life. I kept looking for the father I never had, for a Big Daddy who would take care of me, but all I found was my father over and over—a man who couldn't love anybody."

Faking It

ACOAs put on a good act. At first glance, you wouldn't think we had any problems. Most of us are responsible, dependable, self-sacrificing, hard-working go-getters. Let an emergency rear its head and we can't wait to take care of it.

Vincent Di Pascuale, director of The Starting Point, a counseling center for people with dependency problems, says, "ACOAs do very well in external things, such as achievement, because they're workaholics, they beat themselves to death and they're rigid. You'll find a lot of them in the business world and in production. In fact, an economy such as ours just loves ACOAs because one of them does the work of five other people."

Fran says she likes to help people get through a crisis. "It's funny, but I'm at my best when other people are falling apart. That's when I take over. People look at me and think I've got it all together, and I like that."

But there's a flip side to Fran. "I have needs, just like anybody else, but it's hard for me to ask for help. My friends—even my family—aren't comfortable with me when I can't handle things."

To that, Di Pascuale responds that "what the ACOA can't handle are his feelings. He cuts himself off from what's going on inside of him."

And then what happens?

"Maybe nothing, for a long time," Di Pascuale says. "But eventually he's going to find that he just *can't* do things anymore, and he won't know why."

Steve can remember a time like that a few years ago. "I was in my office. It was late and my wife had just called to find out when I was coming home for dinner, and I bit her head off—not that that was anything new. I bit a lot of heads off, but I knew I could get away with it. I owned the company and I provided very well for my family, so who was going to argue with me? Actually I was a sonofabitch, but boy, did I know how to build a business! I was proud of that, too.

"But that night, after my wife called, I couldn't seem to concentrate. I felt numb—not physically, but emotionally. And hollow. I remember thinking that if I could yell down into the deepest part of myself, I'd get nothing back but an echo. It scared me."

Steve was depressed. He was approaching the point that Vincent Di Pascuale described. He couldn't perform anymore, and it was a terrifying experience.

From the outside, Steve looked like your average solid citizen. He put in long hours, built his business up from scratch, took good care of his wife and daughter, owned a new house in a quiet suburb, drove a substantial but not a flashy car, even helped raise money for an addition to the library. Inside, Steve was another story. He was on his third marriage and it wasn't going well. He had a son from his first marriage and he didn't know how to talk to the boy. He wasn't doing much better with his three-year-old daughter. His wife wanted him to spend more time with his family, but Steve told her it costs money to live well, and you don't make money by sitting home and watching sitcoms.

On paper Steve's business was making a profit, but the employee turnover was very high. Steve was a perfectionist who expected everyone to follow his example. And if he didn't like someone's work, he said so, loud enough for the whole world to hear. If people couldn't take it, tough. They could quit. "A lot of them did," Steve said, "and I just kept telling myself it was the way the world was going. Nobody wanted to work for a buck anymore.

"One night I was saying that to a friend of mine. We were having a few drinks before heading home and I was sounding off. And my friend started telling me I should ease up, maybe give people more of a chance, try to see things their way. I cut him dead. I told him to mind his own business, which, incidentally, wasn't doing all that well, and I left him there. This was a guy I'd known since high school, yet I never wanted to see him again. I figured he didn't really like me and probably was waiting all those years for the right moment to stick a knife in my ribs."

Steve thought of his friend the night he sat at his desk, feeling numb. He wondered how he could turn his back on him. Then he began thinking of his wife. He really didn't want his marriage to end. "I thought of my son and my daughter," he said, "and how we felt so out of sync with each other when we were together. There was so much that was wrong with my life, so many things I wanted to do, but I felt totally impotent. I was a scared kid sitting at a grown man's desk—I felt as if my feet didn't even reach the floor."

Adult children of alcoholics don't feel at home in their own skin. Very often we feel like imposters. And in truth we often are.

Fran puts it this way: "I was one person for my brother and his wife, another for the man I was living with, another for this friend, and yet another for that friend. Sometimes I'd get my roles mixed up and have to do a quick shuffle. But I never was just me."

We're uncomfortable with everyone because we're uncomfortable with ourselves. We know that underneath the adult we're pretending to be, there's a scared, mixed-up child running our life.

Then why don't we ask the child to step aside and let the adult take over? Because the child has been running things for so long that the adult hasn't learned how to take charge. And because the child is afraid to let go, he doesn't trust the adult.

When the Child is in Control

When Steve went into therapy because he was almost paralyzed by fear, he began to see that the child in him was carrying too many burdens and that the adult in him had never developed. The child, in fact, was pretending to be an adult without knowing how, because that's what his alcoholic parents expected of him. And Steve, not yet conscious that there was both a natural child and a natural adult in him who could function separately and appropriately, thought he was a most inept adult. He didn't realize that when a decision had to be made, the child rushed in and made it, leaving the adult in the dust. It was the child who reacted to people and events as if he were always in danger, because that was the way the child always felt. And the best way for the child to deal with danger was to keep it from happening. Consequently the child—in Steve's behalf—tried to control not only his feelings, but everything going on around him. He avoided change of any kind. He never dared be spontaneous, even in congenial surroundings. He was hesitant in his relationships because he didn't want to reveal even the slightest flaw for fear of being rejected. Yes, of course, he tired to be perfect so that no one could criticize him, but he had no patience with anyone else's failings. He thought it was easier for other people to be perfect because they were so much more competent than he was, and when they disappointed him he felt it was another sign of their contempt for him. His touchy outbursts were those of the child insisting that he was, indeed, an adult—and knowing very well he wasn't.

"The kid in me was a brat," Steve says now. And now he can laugh a little when he says it because he has learned how to subdue the child's fear. "I take care of him," he says. What he means is that the adult in him has become strong enough to look after the child.

When the Adult Takes Charge

Something began to happen inside me after I learned to separate the child from the adult. At first, when I began to take care of Little Phyllis, I felt quite awkward. The adult in me was new at her job—she had the talent, all right, but she needed experience.

Dr. DePaula explained that it was not unusual for people to feel that way in the beginning of their split into adult and child. "When you start out, your relationship is an unconscious one. You think you're just one immature adult. It's very hard to begin to see the difference between your child capabilities and your adult capabilities, but after a while you get the hang of it. That's when you can take care of the child."

What surprises me as I look back over that time in my life is that, in taking care of the child in me, I was a much better parent than my own parents had been to me. "Obviously I didn't copy what they did," I said to Dr. DePaula.

"We're only doomed to repeat things if we remain

unaware of them," she said. "That's why it's so important to behave on a conscious level, where we can act on what we know and understand."

I wondered, however, how my natural adult knew how to look after my natural child.

"Children growing up in dysfunctional families are acutely aware of it at an early age," Dr. DePaula explained. "They begin to pay attention to other families. They may think, *I wish I were a kid in that family,* or *I wish that person were my mother,* or *I wish that person were my father.* There's not a whole lot they can do about that while they're children, but when they grow up, they at least have an intellectual awareness of what is better parenting than they got. They may also read newspapers or magazines or books, or see something on TV, that helps them to understand what good parenting is. If they aren't aware that something was wrong with the way they were brought up—if they're into denial—then very likely they'll repeat what was done to them, no matter how much education they've acquired. But if they're living on a conscious level and are aware of the child in them, then they can put their intellectual understanding to work on behalf of their own inner child. Sometimes this doesn't happen until they themselves become parents, and they want their own children to have a genuine childhood. In doing that for their own children, they also do it for the child inside themselves.

"When that happens, it's successful and it feels good. Then something happens to both the natural child and the natural adult; they begin to come together again, but in a different way. A healthy way. The child knows that the adult will look after her, and the adult feels good about doing it. As the adult experiences more of these successes, she becomes more competent."

That's what was happening to me: I was coming together again, but in the right way. My adult was comfortably in charge, and my child was a little girl—for the first time.

Why It's Important to Play

Last year, when the holiday season was underway, I was standing at a cashier's desk in a department store when I noticed that the woman ahead of me was holding a set of four large wooden trains wrapped in a clear plastic bag. "Excuse me," I said, "where did you get those?"

"Over there," she said, pointing to a section of Christmas decorations across the floor. "Aren't they wonderful?"

"Yes," I agreed. The price was right, too. I stood there uncertainly, wondering if I knew a child young enough to enjoy pulling wooden trains around by a long rope. I could think of only one: me.

The trains have been in my living room ever since, quite visible under a coffee table, and my dog and cat no longer express dismay when, every now and then, I pick up the rope and tug the trains around the house like a joyful toddler. Sometimes in my mind I hear voices from my past telling me that I look ridiculous, that a child like me couldn't possibly want anything as useless as a couple of trains and that I'll get tired of them, but I've learned how to tune out those voices. I know now that it's okay for the child in me to have fun because the adult part of me can take care of the serious stuff.

Most of the recovery programs for ACOAs put a lot of emphasis on fun. As Mary Hoffman of Caron Counseling Services explains, "ACOAs don't know how to play. They're busy doing and achieving, and they don't know how to just be." In the Caron ACOA program, every day from 4 to 5 is "playtime," but at first most of the program members would rather avoid it. "Everything an ACOA does has to have a purpose, and some of them will say, 'What's this play shit?' They feel uncomfortable unless they're accomplishing something.

"We explain to them that they can do all kinds of things during playtime—they can take a walk with two or three other people; they can play a board game or even get down on the floor for a game of jacks. We have lots of toys here, and after a while you'll see people taking them down off the shelves and really having a good time doing things they never felt free to do when they were children."

Maybe you're shaking your head the way I did when I pictured myself scampering around a romper room. Maybe you're thinking that if you got along all these years without playing games, you can do without them now. But it's not the games that matter; it's what happens to you when you play them. Learning how to play really does have a purpose. It puts you in touch with emotions you have been denying.

But the way you play is important, too. You may not be able to play at a specified time or because someone says you should. Of course, you can fake it. You're very good at that. You can do what you did as a child: you can pretend to play, and probably you'll get away with it. You may not want to play with other people, at least not in the beginning when it is hard enough to play at all. But you can fake that, too, and if you're in the company of other ACOAs, they may be doing the same thing. Probably you'll all get away with it. And once you're back in your usual routine, you'll stop pretending to have a good time because there's no one around for you to please.

Don't give up on fun. Don't decide that spontaneity, laughter, gregariousness, and enjoyment aren't part of your life. They are bridges to an important part of yourself that you're trying to contact. But maybe you just can't play on command or in a group. Maybe you need to find your own way to have fun. Most children do.

No matter how big your family is, if you're an adult child of an alcoholic, you've been a loner all your life because you didn't feel safe interacting with other people. Now it may be more important for you to learn how to play by yourself before you take on the equally important assignment of playing with others. Besides, having a good time is something we all ought to be able to do—whether we're alone or in a crowd.

I have a wonderful German shepherd dog named Kate, and when she was young I worked with a trainer on basic obedience commands to help Kate fit into my life. As I began to appreciate her intelligence, I thought *Why not see what else she—and I—can do?* We went on to companionship training, protection training, and tracking. As a friend of mine says, "Knowing Kate is like knowing a dog who's gone to graduate school."

Kate seemed so accomplished that I was quite shocked to discover that something important was missing from her life. And from mine, which was no coincidence. Once day when we were visiting Kate's trainer, his wife got down on the floor and played with their own dog, a German shepherd even larger than Kate. The dog and the woman had a great time boxing and wrestling, and I realized that I had never actually played with my dog. If I threw a ball for her, I commanded her to bring it back, sit at my side, and give it to me. If I sent her over the hurdles, I recalled her to my side in a precise manner. I praised her for doing things well, and we enjoyed being with each other, but we didn't do anything just for the fun of it. I was always in control. I was driving Kate toward achievement in the same way I drove myself. I had never been a child with her.

When we came home I decided to play with Kate, but there was nothing spontaneous about it. I crouched on the floor and wondered, *Now what do I do?* (That *has* to be how an ACOA feels being told to play for an hour.) Poor Kate looked at me with her head cocked to one side and a puzzled expression on her face. I made a few feints at her with my hands, trying to get her to box with me, but she licked my face in concern. She barked when I crawled toward her and, my cat, hearing the commotion, sidled into the room to investigate.

Suddenly I realized that I was a typical ACOA trying to achieve a goal: We were going to play a game or bust! I was going to make my dog happy—because all my life I had tried to make everyone I love happy. But this time something was different: *I was able to see what I was doing:*

A. I was pretending to be a child instead of simply being one.
B. I was also pretending to be an adult by making myself do what I thought was expected of me.
C. Until my adult took charge and provided a safe environment, my child could not play.

In the ordinary scheme of things, human beings experience childhood and then go on to experience becoming adults. But in that sense ACOAs aren't ordinary. Our development is arrested early in our lives, and by the time we become aware of our impairment, it is too late to begin again as a child. In order to recover, we must first become an adult, and then we can be a child. In other words, we must first become the parents of ourselves before we can become children.

Let's go back to Kate and me on the floor. . . .

Several things had to take place before the child in me—not the pretender, but the real child—could come forth:

- The adult had to take charge of the situation.
- The adult had to treat the child's fears with compassion.
- The adult had to make the environment safe.
- And then let the child—the real child—go ahead and play.

Developing the Adult

We cannot become adults overnight, but we can at least speed up the process. In order to do this, we need two things that we didn't have earlier in life: some examples and some experiences.

Children usually begin to become adults by following the examples of their parents, and then go on to make their own individual adjustments. If you're an ACOA, you know that the one thing you never wanted to do was follow the example of your parents. You may have gone in the opposite direction, not because it was good for you, but because you thought it was safe.

Doug's father was the alcoholic in the family, but what Doug remembers more clearly than his father's tantrums is his mother's helplessness in dealing with them. "She shouldn't have put up with him, but you know why she did? She never learned to drive. She had to depend on him for everything, as if she were some kind of a prisoner. She couldn't just get in the car and go."

But Doug could. "We lived in a rural area of the South when I was growing up, and kids drive early there. When I was fifteen I bought my first car. It wasn't worth much, only about a hundred dollars, but it ran. I worked on a neighbor's farm for months to earn that money, and when I brought my car home, my father said, 'Did you buy it?'

"I said, 'Yes, I did, with my own money.'

"He didn't say anything then, but it was only a few days after that when he started picking on me at dinner. He used to do that a lot and it would always end up with him beating me up. But that night I wouldn't take it, and he knew it. When he ran into the other room, saying he was going to get his gun, I didn't wait around. I had my car keys in my pocket, and I got out of there. I never went back there to live. I stayed with the family of a friend of mine and I'd go back to see my mother and my sister when I knew my father wasn't around."

Doug drives a truck for a living. His wife is self-sufficient with a responsible supervisory job. He encourages his two daughters to aim at whatever they want, but "to learn how to do it well, so they won't ever have to depend on anyone." Like so many of us, Doug's version of adulthood is to do what his parents weren't able to do. He's made a good life for his family. He's a loving, dependable father, a considerate, stable husband, and a dedicated worker. But the flip side for him is that he can't feel close to people. "There's something that gets in the way," he says.

"I'm okay with my own family," he explains, "but not with anyone else."

Martin feels the same way. "You can use my real name if you want to," he told me when I interviewed

him. "I don't think anybody will recognize me because
. . . well, the truth is, I don't have any friends." Then
he hastened to add, "I'm very happy being with my
family."

If your parents weren't good role models, you don't
have to guess how adults behave. You can find other
examples. You can learn from observing people who
demonstrate the responsibility, compassion, care, and
consistency you'd like to have in a parent. You'll need
to look at all kinds of people; age and gender don't
matter. Keep an open mind. Don't decide ahead of
time how an adult should behave, because you don't
know. Don't look only to one person as your example.
The world is full of people, and you can learn something—either what works or what doesn't—from all of
them.

Hank was the strong man of his ACOA support
group. He was the one everyone else asked for advice.
He's in his early fifties, a big, rangy man with a
street-smart way about him, so he looked the part.
But on the inside he was a frightened child. Until he
was eighteen he was in and out of orphanages because
his alcoholic parents usually couldn't look after him,
so his idea of an adult was someone in authority,
someone rigid, someone not necessarily on his side. He
was afraid of adults, although it took him a long time
to admit it. But, tough guy that he is, once he identi-
fied his fear, he knew he had to overcome it.

"How did you do that?" I asked him.

He gave that some thought. "By paying more attention to people, I guess," he said. "One day I was in a
crowded elevator, with all of us pushed in against
each other, and I was looking straight ahead 'cause I
didn't want to acknowledge that anybody else was
there. I was all locked up inside myself, hiding. I
wasn't even aware that these were other human beings

around me. Then I started looking at the people standing close to me, just a quick glance, and when one of
them looked back at me, I made myself keep looking
at him, even though I felt like saying, 'You sonofabitch,
what're you looking at?'

"Instead, I said something like, 'Pretty crowded, huh?'
and he grunted something back. It was no big deal,
but I felt myself start to relax, and the kid inside me
wasn't so scared. By the time we got down to the main
floor, this guy and I had said a few things back and
forth, and that was all there was to it. We each went
our way. But for me it was a big first step. I actually
got in touch with somebody, and after a while it was
easier for me to talk to other people I didn't know.

"Then I started trying to find out more about
people—I wanted to know what they were like, what
they did with their lives, how they thought and how
they felt. Sometimes they were a lot like me and
sometimes they were different. It didn't matter. The
point is, I was finding out how other people lived. And
when I saw something that looked okay to me, I gave
it a try. I still do that. If I don't like it, I try a different
approach."

Taking Care of the Child

It took me a long time to begin to become an adult,
and, like Hank, I followed the example of people who
seemed to know what they were doing. Sometimes I
was wrong about them, and sometimes what worked
for them didn't work for me. But perhaps the most
important thing I learned during that time of intense
experimentation is that an adult can make mistakes.

I don't have to be perfect. I don't have to know all
the answers. I don't have to be afraid of change. I can

take life as it comes. I can face up to its difficulties and enjoy its pleasures. I don't have to do things in the same way all the time. I can be flexible. But I do have to be consistent in being an adult. I can't be in charge of my life one moment, and the next moment turn it over to the child. In fact, I can't turn anything over to the child, ever, because the child isn't capable of running my life. I'm the one who has to take care of the child, not the other way around.

"I still slip up every now and then," Elizabeth admits. "Something happens—with the kids, at work, with a friend—and my child comes running in to help. And right away I get that kind of sick, anxious feeling in the pit of my stomach that tells me, 'Oh-oh, she's at it again!'

"When I was growing up I was always trying to fix things for people, and it's hard to break that habit. Maybe a friend isn't getting along with her husband, or my son isn't working on his term paper, and right away I try to put their lives in order. That's stupid, and I know it. At least *now* I know it—and now I can do something about it."

What does she do?

"Usually, all I have to do is ask myself one question: *Do I have any business here?* And as soon as I say that, I feel as if I'm in charge again. I'm an adult, and if people really need my help—if I can really do something—I'll do it. But if I'd just be getting in the way, then I don't."

How does she get the child out of the way?

"Gently," Elizabeth says. "Lovingly. Again, it helps me to say something to her, something like, 'Here, why don't you sit over here and look at some of these coloring books. I'll take care of this problem.'"

How does the child respond?

"With great relief!" Elizabeth says. "By now she's beginning to trust me. She knows I can take care of her. She doesn't come running in half as much as she used to."

Getting back once more to Kate and me trying to have fun . . .

As soon as my adult took charge of the situation I became aware of my child's needs. I realized I was trying to make her do something that wasn't comfortable for her. Getting down on the floor and boxing wasn't my child's idea of fun and never would be. She enjoys the long hikes I take with Kate along a wooded trail bordering a lake near my home, but she wasn't sure that would qualify as "having a good time."

I'm like Elizabeth in that I find it helpful to discourse with the child in me. "Of course, it does," I told her. "The point is, I want *you* to have a good time, so it helps to know what you like to do."

But would that make Kate happy? she wondered.

"Neither one of us can *make* Kate happy," I said. "But we can love her and take good care of her—and I think we do."

I have always enjoyed walking in the woods with my dog, but that afternoon the experience was special. I felt as if a young child was accompanying us, and I began to see the landscape through her eyes. I noticed how many different kinds of trees there were, and how the flicker of sunlight gave texture to the lake water. I laughed at a rascally squirrel that waited until just the right moment to invite Kate on a chase she couldn't hope to win. I took a few detours I normally didn't take. I threw some sticks for Kate and we startled two fishermen in a rowboat close to shore, who scowled at us for making so much noise.

I was in charge. I had created a safe playground in the midst of my life where the child in me felt free to be herself. I was having a wonderful time. I was having fun.

When I described that experience to Dr. DePaula,

she said, "As you go back and let your child have a more normal childhood, some of the old wounds begin to heal. They don't keep coming up and getting in your way all the time. But you also gain access to the joyfulness of the child, and that was never available to you before. There had been terror, sadness, depression, fear, hurt, and lack of self-esteem. But joyfulness? —where was that unbounded joy and creativity of the child? I don't want to idealize this concept because it's really very practical. But little children have a wonder and a curiosity and a joy about the world—if they haven't been trampled. And that's something you can get back in touch with by taking really good care of the child."

As our adult gains more experience taking charge of our life, she will become more competent and the child will become more trusting. And as the adult begins to provide the nurturing atmosphere a child needs, the child will stop looking for love where she can't ever hope to get it. She will look to the adult instead, and she will not be disappointed. She will depend on the adult to seek out healthy relationships where love is exchanged rather than withheld. She will discover how good it feels just to be. In time, the two of them— the childlike child and the competent, caring adult— will grow together into a whole, functioning, loving, and lovable person.

CHAPTER THREE

GUILT AND RESPONSIBILITY

WHEN YOU SIT IN on a group of ACOAs sharing their experiences, the two words you hear most often are *guilt* and *responsibility*—in that order. There's a connection between them, and a reason for the order. The child of an alcoholic parent grows up believing that he is the cause of his parent's problems, so he tries to relieve his guilt by solving them. He blames himself for everything that is wrong and tries to make everything right, and he goes on to repeat this pattern of guilt and responsibility in his other relationships. He becomes a fixer, martyr, burden-bearer, and patsy. He demands perfection of himself, yet he allows dependent, irresponsible people to lean on him until his knees buckle. And the guilt remains. Because the ACOA doesn't know how it got there in the first place, he can't get rid of it.

When Fran was about ten years old, her father beat her mother for the first time. The three of them were sitting at the kitchen table, eating dinner. Fran's father had been drinking heavily ever since he came home from work, which wasn't unusual.

"He drank moonshine," Fran remembers. "That's strong stuff. He used to get real nasty when he was drunk, so my mother and I were being careful not to say or do anything to make him mad. My mother never talked back to him or anything like that, but he'd try to pick a fight with her. Then he'd call her names.

"But this one night he started hitting my mother, and I got scared. I started to cry, but the more I cried, the more he hit my mother. He kept telling her, 'See, you're making her cry!' The next day my mother told me that if he ever hit her again, I shouldn't cry. She said, 'That only makes it worse for me.' I felt as if it was my fault.

"It did happen again a few weeks later, and again after that. My mother was everything to me, and seeing her get hurt was bad enough. But knowing that if I cried, she'd suffer even more—it was horrible. While my father was hitting my mother, I'd make myself go right on eating as if I didn't see anything. I didn't cry. I don't know how I didn't, but after that, it was very hard for me to cry at all about anything.

"Up until that first time my father beat my mother, I had been a pretty ordinary little girl. But all of a sudden my whole life changed. It was the end of my childhood, for one thing. I felt as if I had a big burden to carry, because I had to keep everything on an even keel. Before that, I used to try to get out of things like setting the table or doing my homework, but after I saw my father do that, I became the best little girl you ever saw. I had to be.

"It changed my relationship with my father, too. Until then I loved him. I used to think he was the sweetest, most fun-loving man in the world, but that was all gone. I was afraid of him. My father never hit me. He didn't have to, because I could see what he was capable of doing. He hurt me in other ways."

Although there often is physical and sexual abuse in the families of alcoholics, the greatest amount of abuse is emotional. The example Fran gave is especially graphic: She blamed herself for her father's brutality, and she felt responsible for stopping it. "My father and my brother didn't get along at all, but I could usually put my father in a good mood. He'd always want me to go along with him when he drove down to the store or to get gas, and I'd go. I don't think he even suspected how much I hated him then, because I was so nice to him. I was always his sweet little girl.

"When I was a little older, I tried to talk my mother into leaving him. She was afraid to do that because he told her that if she ever left him, he'd find her and kill her. But I used to say, 'He won't do that. We'll go someplace where he'll never find us, and we'll both get jobs and live in a nice apartment by ourselves.' I begged her to do it, and one time she did. She took me with her to her sister's house, but she didn't have a job or any money, so we had to go back. My mother wouldn't leave after that, but running away was a dream of mine for most of my childhood. I wouldn't have gone on my own, not without my mother."

Playing the Alcoholic's Game

For many years I had a very confused relationship with my mother. I either loved her in a way that excluded everything else in my life, or I hated her passionately. And either way, I felt guilty. My love never made her happy, and my hatred made her suffer. We were either very close, or I stayed away from her, sometimes for years. Yet even when I didn't see her, I always felt that she could rattle my chains at will and from any distance.

I can't tell you how many hours I spent in therapy, going over and over each and every move I had made while I was growing up, always trying to answer the nagging question: Had I done the right thing? I never felt that I had, at least not completely. Sometimes in my mind I could justify my behavior and feelings, but even then, there was always the uncomfortable inner conviction that somehow I had been wrong. What I didn't realize—partly because it seemed so bizarre, and still does—was that I was *supposed* to feel wrong. It was illogical and undeserved, yet it was the foundation of my relationship with my mother.

It wasn't until several years ago, when I came across *Games People Play*, Eric Berne's classic book on transactional analysis, that I began to understand why I was supposed to feel wrong: It is part of the game an alcoholic plays. As Dr. Berne explained, his use of the word *game* refers to the alcoholic's interaction with other people; it has no relationship to the debate over alcoholism as a disease: "If a biochemical or physiological abnormality is the prime mover in excessive drinking—and that is still open to some question—then its study belongs in the field of internal medicine. Game analysis is interested in something quite different—the kinds of social transactions that are related to such excesses."

This is an important distinction for any ACOA who feels that his attitude toward his alcoholic parents is complicated, and in many ways thwarted, because alcoholism is classified as a disease by the American Medical Association. You can't help feeling guilty when you're angry about someone who is sick, and this additional guilt only exaggerates your anger because it has nowhere to go. But it clears the head to realize that the disease, if it is a disease, is something to be treated by medical scientists. The *behavior* of the person with the disease is something that has to be confronted by the people it affects.

Any ACOA knows the frustration of trying to make an alcoholic parent happy—and continually failing. Any ACOA knows the agony of believing it is his fault when the parent *isn't* happy. We blame ourselves for doing something wrong, or for not loving enough. Some of us blame a parent's unhappiness on the fact that we exist, and we spend our lives trying to make up for the misery that event supposedly causes. All the time we are missing the point of this strange parent-child relationship: *The alcoholic does not want to be loved and does not want to be happy. The alcoholic wants to be punished, and he wants us to make it happen.*

As Dr. Berne explained, ". . . the *payoff* in 'Alcoholic' (as is characteristic of games in general) comes from the aspect to which most investigators pay least attention. In the analysis of this game, drinking itself is merely an incidental pleasure having added advantages, the procedure leading up to the real culmination, which is the hangover . . . For the Alcoholic the hangover is not as much the physical pain as the psychological torment."

The aim of the game, according to Berne, is self-castigation. "The main conversational interest of many alcoholics in the therapeutic situation is not their drinking, which they apparently mention most in deference to their persecutors, but their subsequent suffering. The transactional object of the drinking, aside from the personal pleasures it brings, is to set up a situation where the [Alcoholic's] Child can be severely scolded, not only by the [Alcoholic's] internal Parent, but by any parental figures in the environment who are interested enough to oblige."

Dr. Claude Steiner, a colleague of Dr. Berne and the author of *Games Alcoholics Play*, takes this aim a step further: ". . . just as people explore their social context in search of persons who fit into their games, so do persons who have scripts which involve the use of drugs search for the drug which fits their life plan. Alcohol addiction involves gradual, long-term self-destruction of a socially acceptable sort."

Drinking is a means to that end. But the alcoholic doesn't simply take a drink and then keep on drinking until he is drunk or passes out or both. In his own mind he needs a reason to drink, and the range of reasons is vast. He can take a drink because someone offended him, or because someone didn't appreciate him. He can take a drink because someone suggested he ought to cut down on his drinking (and who the hell does he think *he* is!). He can take a drink because someone is silent (and who knows what that sonofabitch might be thinking!). Or because someone talks too much (the noise!). He can take a drink because there is a reason to celebrate (he got a raise, he bought a new car, it's a beautiful day!). One young man remembers his alcoholic father drinking especially heavily whenever he was in the company of a man taller than he was because he didn't like being short.

Finding a reason to drink is only the beginning of the alcoholic's game. He must then drink to excess and finally be punished for it by suffering deep remorse and self-debasement, often in the form of a hangover and a shattered relationship. The punishment itself can serve as a compelling reason to start drinking all over again. The alcoholic's self-castigation, however, is not the ultimate end of the game. It serves another more subtle but most important purpose. As Dr. Steiner explains it, "... the Alcoholic transacts from an existential position exemplified by the sentence 'I'm no good and you're O.K. (ha, ha)' ... [he] puts himself in a position of being obviously disapproved of, allowing those who disapprove to appear virtuous and blameless when the situation, closely examined, shows that they are not only not virtuous and blameless, but foolish and full of blame. Thus, 'I'm no good, you're O.K. (ha, ha)' really means 'You're not O.K.,' but stated in such a way that everyone will be utterly confused."

Describing an incident in which an alcoholic husband is berated by his wife (who is playing the role of Persecutor), Dr. Steiner says, ". . . he [the alcoholic] always has a smile on his face [when his wife berates him], and he always says [to himself], 'I'll show you it's not really that way; you're the one who's not O.K.' That is why, with 'Alcoholic,' as with other games, it is often important to watch the smiles of the player because they frequently reveal where the payoff is." How well I played this game, and how clearly I remember those peculiar smiles.

"The important thing to remember, once again, is that the payoff of alcoholism, suicide, and other self-destructive behavior is the effect of this behavior on others," Dr. Steiner writes.

"Alcoholism" is a game that can't be played alone. It requires other players: the person who provides the reason to drink, the one who supplies the drink, the one who accuses the alcoholic of drinking too much (and thereby reinforces the reason to drink), the one who tries to save the alcoholic from destroying himself (and *must* be disappointed, *but* at the appropriate moment), and the one who tells him, in no uncertain terms the next morning, that he's a no-good S.O.B. If the game is played successfully, the alcoholic feels thoroughly punished—yet triumphant—and is ready to demonstrate his unworthiness once again, if possible with the same players.

And what do the players get out of all this? Besides the pain and disappointment, they often feel as if they aren't sane. Somewhere in the deeper layers of the alcoholic's psyche, the game makes sense, possibly because it achieves what the alcoholic set out to do, but the players don't understand what is going on. All they know is that they continually go after the same lures in whatever form they are offered, and they repeatedly fail to accomplish what they set out to do, which was to love the alcoholic and save him from himself.

Why We keep Playing

When two people marry, they bring their separate histories together. If all goes well, they will be able to satisfy their own and each other's needs, but if their needs are unhealthy, they will play games with each other. Yet each of them has a past to remember; there are situations and events they can compare to the way they live now. If something is wrong with their relationship, they may not know how to fix it, but at least they sense it is wrong.

But a child doesn't have a past, and if his parent is an alcoholic, he is caught up in the parent's game from the time he is born. He has no way of realizing that the relationship itself may be wrong; he thinks *he* is wrong and he keeps trying to make up for it. Sometimes, if there aren't enough other people available, he'll even play more than one part in the parent's game—because the parent seems to go to pieces if he doesn't, and the child doesn't want that guilt added to the guilt he already has. And even though the odds are against it, he is still trying to strengthen his parent in anticipation of the day when his parent will finally take care of him.

When my mother was sober, we had some wonderful

times together. She could be warm, affectionate, inventive, and patient. She taught me how to read and write before I was old enough to go to school, and I remember so vividly the hours she would spend with me, going over the alphabet and putting letters together to form words. Her pleasure in my achievement made me an eager student. Almost every weekday night she would make up a new bedtime story for me, and there are some that I remember almost word for word. I felt loved at those times.

But when Friday night arrived, she withdrew from me as if I weren't there. She spent most of her time with her friends, either going out with them or giving parties for them in our apartment, and they all drank a lot. At those times, she had absolutely no interest in anything I did or said, and if I tried to get her attention by pulling out some of the words I had written during the week, she found fault with them. She would tell me she praised them only because she wanted to be a good mother, but now she was tired of trying to be a good mother. If I showed how hurt I felt, she became furious. She would describe in detail the sacrifices she had made for me and tell me how hard it was for such a young woman to be burdened with a child. She blamed me for her divorce from my father; she said he didn't want me. She blamed me because she wasn't married again; the men she dated didn't want me, either.

That's a long tirade for a child to hear, and I was to hear it for years, even after my mother remarried. I was too young to take in a lot of it, but eventually the underlying message got through to me: My mother drank because she was unhappy, and I was the reason why she was unhappy. The very fact that I existed made me a player in her game. All she had to do was look at me to make it okay for her to begin drinking, and she could continue drinking by remembering how hard she worked at being a mother that week. All I had to do to feel guilty was see her drinking. I blamed myself for it. If she told me again how much I was costing her in terms of happiness, I turned my anger on myself and felt sorry for her.

The one role I never was able to play was that of the drink supplier, probably because I saw alcohol as the villain and myself as my mother's rescuer. Besides, there were many others available for that part in the game. I used to hate them for offering my mother the very substance that was destroying her. Later I began to see that they were trying to win her love, just as I was, but in different ways. Some of them were ignorant of my mother's alcoholism, and some had their own reasons for denying the truth. My stepfather, a less obvious alcoholic, was my mother's greatest, most enduring supplier. For all the years they were married, he mixed her drinks, served them frequently, stocked their liquor cabinet, and took her out to drink. It was what kept them together, and only recently did I realize that he was always afraid she would leave him.

Although I couldn't be a supplier, I played the other roles in the game very well. Pretending to be an adult, I lectured my mother fervently about the dangers of drinking—and of course provided her with another reason to do so. If she expressed even the slightest willingness to change her behavior, I became her rescuer, armed with all sorts of advice about kicking the habit. And when she seemed to welcome my interest and heed the advice, but then got drunk again, I was only too ready the next morning to add to the pain of her hangover by telling her, in detail, what she had done the night before and didn't remember.

I didn't like playing any of those parts; I doubt that

anyone does. When my parents—once the game was over and before a new one began—called me "a pill," "a prude," "spiteful," "ungrateful," "a judge," and "the little cop," I had to agree with them. I thought I was a terrible person—and with sufficient reason. The game called for me to be terrible, and I was involved in the game almost all of the time. If there were any redeeming qualities in my makeup, I had little opportunity to discover them. Self-esteem in a child is unacceptable to the alcoholic parent, perhaps because it interferes with the playing of the game.

Some of Us Drop Out

Not every child of an alcoholic stays in the game. Some drop out and some don't attempt to play at all. They are not necessarily better off; they may be in much deeper trouble.

In any description of a typical ACOA, a lot of attention is given to our need for approval. This leads people to assume that we're all very agreeable—and some of us aren't. Some of us just give up trying to win a parent's love. We don't even look for love anywhere else. We think so little of ourselves, and our expectations are so low, that we try to do without being loved because we don't think we have any chance of getting it.

"I gave up trying to please my old man when I was thirteen," Paul said. "I used to get good grades, I never got into trouble, I knew how to tiptoe around my father so he wouldn't blow up. But none of that mattered. He'd still find something wrong with me and beat me, sometimes so bad I wound up in the hospital.

"Finally, I said to myself, 'Why bother? Why try?'

My two brothers didn't try half as hard as I did, and my old man treated them better. I started cutting school. I didn't do my homework. Sure, my grades went down, and I barely made it through high school. But my father still beat me up, so nothing I did made any difference.

"I got to be a real mean guy. If anybody looked at me for more than a second, I'd be ready to punch him out—in fact, I looked forward to it. I had so much anger in me I just had to hit something. I ended up hurting myself more than anybody, but I didn't care."

Paul still looks formidable. He's a big-boned man with thick gray-black hair and a massive beard, and he speaks in short, forceful sentences. "I was lucky," he says. "Before I was eighteen, I got into so much trouble that a judge told my parents either I go to jail or go to a psychiatrist. I was all for going to jail, but I think my old man just wanted to spite me, so he actually paid for me to go to a doctor.

"I didn't go for long. As soon as I was eighteen, I quit and joined the navy. But even that little bit of counseling helped. It gave me a different look at myself. It got some of the anger out of me and I stopped fighting."

Paul had started drinking in his teens. "I could drink all night and never get drunk. I was real proud of that because I thought I was showing my old man I was tougher than he was. But it caught up with me, and one day I got roaring drunk and couldn't even remember what happened. That scared me right into AA. Then, after I stopped drinking, I went into Al-Anon, because that's where they deal with people who come from alcoholic families. I didn't know about ACOAs until then, but as soon as I found out what it meant, I began to understand what happened to me."

Paul is active in several ACOA recovery groups,

and he's the kind of man others look to for leadership. He listens sympathetically when another child of an alcoholic talks about the past, and very quickly he will interrupt when someone expresses shame about the behavior of a parent. "Hey, that's nothing new!" he'll tell her. "You're among friends—we all know how it feels to grow up in a nuthouse. The trouble with you is, you thought you were the only one whose family was crazy!"

Paul still doesn't socialize outside the groups. "I'm okay with other ACOAs," he says, "but I feel out of place anywhere else."

Why?

"It's a lot of hard work getting to know somebody. I guess I'm just not very optimistic that it will work out."

Undoubtedly Paul has raised his expectations to the point where he can admit some friendships into his life. But only a few. And only under certain circumstances. He doesn't want to risk getting caught up in any more games.

Jerry never made it that far. He was the youngest of six children. By the time he was born, his alcoholic father's health was so deteriorated that he couldn't play the game well. All he wanted was a reason to drink, and Jerry was a convenient scapegoat. "I guess I was stupid or something," Jerry said. "I didn't do well in school—my brothers and sisters were straight-A."

"It wasn't Jerry's fault," his older brother says. "My father used to stand over him every night while he did his homework and look for mistakes. Jerry was afraid to write 2 and 2. That was when he was in grade school. By the time he got to high school, he was flunking out. He still couldn't read, but he was such a nice kid, the teachers kept passing him with D's. That's all my father had to see—D's. He'd take one look at

Jerry's report card and tear it up. Then he'd pull out a bottle of scotch and drink until he passed out."

Jerry didn't finish school. He dropped out during his junior year and hung out. He drank too much and was into drugs. A month after he got his driver's license, he totaled a car and lost his license for two years. "He didn't do anything except sit in his room and look out the window, waiting for his friends to come and pick him up," his mother says. "I don't understand what happened to him—he was the sweetest child you ever saw. He's still sweet in his own way, but he just doesn't seem to be there when you talk to him."

Jerry's father died a year ago. Now Jerry lives at home with his mother, but his brothers and sisters have moved out. He has a job in a factory and never misses a day of work. When he comes home, he always brings a six-pack and finishes it after dinner in his room. His friends don't come around anymore and he doesn't go out.

This is the kind of ACOA we don't read about because he doesn't show up in studies and recovery programs. He doesn't think enough of himself to ask for help, so we don't know how many more like him are out there. We know only a few things about him, and they don't fit into the typical ACOA profile. For instance, he is not eager to please, although he won't do anything to arouse your anger, either. He is not a workaholic or an overachiever; he does only what is required to stay alive. He isn't looking for love because he doesn't think there is any. He doesn't attempt to have relationships, so he isn't bothered by an inability to get close or an excessive amount of loyalty. He doesn't struggle with guilt and responsibility; he was overcome by them a long time ago. Withdrawal may be his way of saying he's been hurt too much, and he'd like to be left alone now, please.

Repeating the Past

Most children of alcoholics think life will be different for them once they get away from their parents, but it rarely is. They seem to go looking for people who make them feel guilty and responsible, and the game goes on in other relationships. Of course they meet other kinds of people, but they aren't comfortable with them because they don't know how to behave if they can't accommodate someone else's needs and deny their own.

Claire is a twenty-two-year-old single mother of two young children. Her father was an alcoholic who deserted the family when Claire was two. Her mother got a divorce and married again, this time to a man who didn't drink. "He was a 'dry' alcoholic," Claire explains. "He behaved just like an alcoholic even though he never got drunk. He was obnoxious and temperamental. I hated him."

Claire's mother didn't drink, but her father, Claire's grandfather, was an alcoholic. "My mother and my grandmother were caretakers. That isn't going to happen to me," she says.

When Claire was thirteen, her stepfather began abusing her sexually. "I told one of my teachers, and she reported it to the Family Court," she says. "Then some social workers started coming around. After that, I was always in some kind of counseling program."

Claire became pregnant at sixteen and gave birth to a daughter. She refused to name the father. "My stepfather threw me out, and I went to live with my father. He was in AA then and wasn't drinking, so we got along pretty well." Claire finished high school, took a secretarial course, and got a job. Then she married a young man named David and had a son by him.

"I didn't know it until after we got married, but David was an alcoholic. He was on drugs, too.

"I've always believed that the family should come first. But David put drinking and drugs ahead of me and the kids. When I threatened to leave him, he promised to change. And he did, in a way. He joined AA and stopped drinking, but then he put his AA group ahead of me and the kids. When he used to drink, he was never home—and when he stopped drinking, he was out all the time with his support group. So all the craziness was still there. Sometimes the baby would have to go to the hospital, or I'd be sick, and David would be at an AA dance.

"We had different priorities. I put the kids and him first. He put sobriety first—which I could handle—then his job, then his support group, then me and the kids."

Claire went to Al-Anon for a while, and it helped. "They proved to me that I was an enabler, just like my mother and grandmother. But I stopped going because David went to four meetings a week and somebody had to stay home and be with the kids. Finally I took the kids and left."

Now Claire lives with another young man but refuses to marry him. "I'll never get married again," she says. "I don't want to get trapped." She's gone as far as she can in her present job and she's looking for something with better prospects. By the time she's twenty-five, Claire hopes to find a way to go back to school. "I need more education if I want to take better care of myself and my children."

Listening to Claire, I had the feeling that she was starting to break away from the pattern of being a player in the alcoholic's game—until she began to talk about Kenny, whom she calls "my roommate."

"I didn't want to get involved with a man again," she began, "but the truth is, I needed someone to help foot the bills. And Kenny's different. He understands how I feel about my kids, and he cares about them, too. He's not on drugs, and he doesn't drink. Well, not really very much. I work weekends in a cocktail bar, and Kenny'll come in about an hour before I finish work. They have a band there, and he knows I like to dance, so if there aren't many customers around at that hour, we get to have some fun. He'll have a few drinks at the bar while he's waiting for me to finish up, but he gets them at half price, and he always knows when to stop. A couple of times he got drunk, but he knows how I feel about that and he really was sorry.

"Kenny has a good job. He's a mechanic, and he works near home so he gets home early. Usually he stops at a bar on the way and has a few drinks with his friends, but he's home in time for dinner. I always know where he is because he doesn't have a car and he has to call me to come and get him. I take him to work in the morning, too, so I know where he is. Sometimes he asks, Why can't he use my car and drive me to work? but I tell him, 'Oh, no, not after what happened to *your* car!' He totaled his last year on New Year's Eve. He had a little too much—you know how it is on New Year's. But I'm not going to let him do that to *my* car!"

Somehow, much of what Claire said sounded familiar. She was still feeling very negative about herself and making excuses for someone else.

Elizabeth remembers how hard she tried to avoid marrying her first husband. They met when she was in college and he was in law school. "After we started dating, I realized I didn't feel comfortable with him. He was so manipulative and critical of me. But every time I tried to break it off, he got very upset and angry. Or else, he'd cry on my shoulder and I'd feel sorry for him because he really seemed to care about me. When he finished law school he wanted to get engaged, and I didn't think it was fair for me to say no after all the time we'd been going together. Then I didn't know what to do, because for some reason I just didn't want to marry him.

"My best friend used to beg me to break off the engagement. She said, 'I'll go with you to tell him, if you don't want to do it alone. And I'll help you send back all the wedding gifts. I'll wrap them, I'll write the notes, I'll do anything! Just don't marry Stan! You're so wrong for each other.'

"Well, I did break the engagement, and he was furious with me, but somehow I stuck to my decision. I went back to school soon after that, so we didn't see each other for a long time. But Stan used to write to me—such thoughtful letters, so considerate and caring. He was such a wonderful letter-writer that I began to forget how domineering he was. When I came home for the holidays, we spent a lot of time together and he was so nice to me! He told me he still loved me and wanted to get engaged again.

"After I was back at school I found out I was pregnant and I panicked. I called Stan and he said I shouldn't worry, he'd marry me. It wouldn't be a big wedding, he said, but he wanted to do what was right. He didn't say anything about loving me then, but I didn't think there was anything wrong with that. I was so *grateful* to him! It was his child, but I thought, *He doesn't know that for sure.* I didn't even want to think about the mess I'd be in if my parents found out I was pregnant, with no husband in sight.

"When I hung up the phone I promised myself that I would never give Stan a single minute's regret for marrying me. And I kept that promise. I damned near died doing it, too. He was never considerate, thoughtful, or caring again, but I didn't complain. I tried to be exactly the kind of wife and mother he wanted. With three children born close together, it's hard to keep a house even halfway decent, but I tried to keep it spotless because that's the way Stan wanted it to be. I was hoping to go back to school part-time, and get my degree, and we could have afforded a baby-sitter for a few hours a week, but Stan wouldn't hear of it. He wanted me to be with the children all the time. He didn't even want me to see my friends because he didn't like them. But if he invited sixteen of his lawyer friends and their wives to dinner, he expected me to whip up an elegant meal on short notice. He was critical of everything—the way I dressed, the way I talked, everything!

"I have to say this in his defense: I never stood up for myself. I never made a case for going to school or being with my own friends. I can't even remember *thinking* about anything like that because what I needed didn't occur to me. I was a blank page. The only thing that mattered was pleasing Stan because he married me when I was pregnant. And I couldn't seem to do anything to please him.

"I know this sounds strange, but I was miserable and didn't know it. I'd try to talk myself into being happy and then I'd feel guilty because I wasn't. Actually I was very depressed and didn't realize it. I'd wake up in the morning and I wouldn't want to get out of bed. I can't say I wanted to kill myself, because I didn't have the courage to do something like that. But I didn't want to go on living, and I was wishing something would make me stop."

Elizabeth had a breakdown when her oldest child was four years old. "It was all very hush-hush. Stan sent me to a mental hospital and told the children that 'Mommy went away.' I was there for a long, long time before I began to respond to the therapy. I had covered up my own needs so well that it took a while to dig down and find them. I guess Stan lost patience with me because when he came to see me one day, he said, 'You're of no use to me like this.' Then he told me he was divorcing me and taking custody of our children. I didn't know what to say. All I could do was nod my head. I guess I was still trying to please him."

Changing the Way We Look at Ourselves

ACOAs are urged to get rid of their guilt, but no one tells us how. "Detach," some of the recovery programs advise us, and by that they mean we should stop allowing ourselves to get hooked by other people's needs. However, it's easy for ACOAs to interpret "detach" to mean we shouldn't allow ourselves to feel, and we can easily use it as an excuse to continue avoiding close relationships. We've been doing that for most of our lives, with the result that we have become detached from ourselves rather than from the alcoholic. If anything, we need to acknowledge our feelings instead of denying that we have any; they are a necessary part of healthy relationships.

"Detach" for the ACOA is roughly the equivalent of "Just say no" in some anti-drug programs: it speaks to the intellect rather than the emotions. It offers no opportunity for us to understand why we ever felt the need to play the alcoholic's game, and it assumes we can change a deeply emotional response by repeating words and phrases that make sense to the mind. It may even persuade us that we can, with care, avoid playing alcoholic games forever, very much the way the recovering alcoholic avoids getting drunk by not drinking. It doesn't prepare us for the times when we don't see a game coming and suddenly find ourselves back in the middle of it.

I think ACOAs can do better than to detach. I think we should be able to take a good look at the alcoholic's game, see it for what it is, and feel no compulsion to play. But before we can do that, we have to break free of the pattern of guilt and responsibility.

We forget that a lot of what we did as children was normal, loving, and a healthy response to an unhealthy situation. We don't see ourselves that way now because we were repeatedly told we were wrong, and that perception of ourselves has stayed with us. Even as adults we continue to look at ourselves through our parents' eyes, and everything about us looks wrong. To correct that faulty perception, we have to go back to the child we were, look at him or her through our own eyes, and draw our own conclusions about the kind of person we really are.

A few years ago I had a painful but illuminating insight into the way we can change our negative perception of ourselves. Since my mother died, my stepfather and I continue to see each other occasionally, and we get along fairly well, for two reasons: We never talk about anything important, and I no longer ask him for something he can't give me. We talk more often by telephone and one day, shortly before I was going to visit him, he told me he was drinking and smoking less. I had given up trying to persuade him to do that years ago, so when he decided to do it on his own, I thought, *At last!*

When I arrived at his home, I gave him a big hug and said, "Gee, I'm glad to see you, Dad!"

He grunted curtly and said, "That would be nice if you meant it." Then he busied himself with closing the door.

I was stunned. He didn't seem to notice it and went on talking about nothing in particular. How was the traffic? Did I stop to eat? Was everything all right at home? He gave me no chance to answer any of his questions, but even if he had, I couldn't have done it. Something terrible was going on in me.

I was back in my childhood—not by way of my imagination, but actually. I felt as if I had done something wrong by saying I was glad to see him. It was an honest emotion, an expression of love, and it was rejected as phony. The rejection even made me *feel* phony. So many years had passed since anything like that had happened between me and my mother or my step-father. In the meantime I had grown up and built a worthwhile life for myself. I had recovered from some of my ACOA problems, and it was a shock to find out that I was still vulnerable. Once again I had been conned into believing that my alcoholic parent was going to change, and I went running in to give him encouragement. And once again I found myself playing the game, providing him with a reason to drink—sure enough, he went to the refrigerator for a beer! Before the adult in me could do anything about it, the child in me was hooked into thinking, *Oh, look what I made him do!* All my years of hard work, all the therapy, all the people who had helped me to see myself as a person of value—it was all gone in that moment. I felt worthless, unloved, and unloving. I was afraid I was going to die, somehow.

It was the child in me who felt devastated, but the adult in me knew it—that was the single most important difference between what was happening to me then and what used to happen to me a long time ago. As Dr. DePaula explained to me recently, "When a person becomes conscious of the child and also more competent as an adult, she begins to appreciate that, in certain situations, the hurt she feels is really the hurt of the child." This time my adult could do something about the hurt I felt. What, I didn't know, but I began to think, *How can I help my unhappy child?*

For a little while, I stalled. My stepfather settled in a chair and talked about baseball, TV, and what we might eat for dinner. I could listen to him without hearing, because he wasn't interested in my responses, and I had more important matters on my mind. I considered detaching, which would have meant cutting the visit short and going home. But that wouldn't have made my child stop feeling wrong about herself, and that was the situation I had to address. The adult in me was putting my needs first—quite a change from the past.

On the coffee table I noticed an old photograph album I hadn't seen in a long time, and I began leafing through it idly while my stepfather was looking through his desk drawers for a letter he wanted to show me. And suddenly I came upon a picture of myself when I was five, a black-and-white enlargement of a snapshot taken by a neighbor. I hadn't seen pictures of myself as a child in years—hadn't wanted to, because I didn't like that part of my life—and perhaps because this one was large and I came upon it so unexpectedly, I felt as if I were looking at someone else's child. My immediate reaction was that I liked her, and I held on to that feeling. I saw character in the eyes, and decency, even a gentle spirituality. It's the way all children are, I think, and I realized that I was that way, too.

I was seeing the child I had been through my own eyes, the eyes of the adult I had become. She was very different from the child my parents told me I was.

Then I began to remember snatches of incidents from long ago, incidents that told me more about the child I really was. I remembered standing up to a truly nasty woman who lived across the street, next door to my best friend's house. She was shouting racial obscenities at my friend for trying to retrieve a ball that landed in her shrubbery, and I told her she couldn't do that because it was against the law. I could identify with that child because I would do the same thing today.

I remembered walking a neighbor's dog, an elderly fox terrier I used to pretend was mine, and picking her up just as another dog, unleashed, made a lunge at her. I got a small bite on my left arm, which the two dog owners made a fuss about, but the fox terrier was safe and that's all that mattered to me. I'd do that same thing today, too.

Looking at that photograph, I liked having been that child. I began to feel a parent's love for her. I could see quite clearly that I was not a wrong little kid—nor is any other child—and I did not grow up to be a wrong person. I loved my mother and my stepfather. I wanted to help them get well. I wanted them to love me. There was nothing wrong with any of those emotions. Telling me I was wrong to feel that way was wrong. Calling my love a lie was wrong. Manipulating my emotions to lure me into a game was wrong. I had been a *wounded* child, but I could be healed. So can we all. Given a little time, we all can correct our vision of ourselves by looking at the child we were through our adult eyes.

I didn't cut my visit short. There was no reason to do that. I no longer felt worthless and unloved. In fact, I felt pretty good about myself. I kept my child very close to me, imagining that I could feel her snuggle close to me for the support she knew she would get from me. She was safe from anything my stepfather might say, so there was no need for me to feel anxious.

Ever since that visit, I have had better times with my stepfather. I think it's because I allow my adult to interact with him, but never my child. The terms of our relationship are far too complicated for Little Phyllis to comprehend. My adult can understand that this man cannot give me the love I needed as a child, and neither can he accept the love I have for him. But I am loved in other ways now, and there will be even more in the future. As for the love I have for him, that's for my adult and not my child to offer, and it will always be there. My stepfather doesn't have to take it to prove that I am capable of love. I know I am, and so does my child—and that's what counts.

Occasionally my stepfather—and a few other people— can still take me by surprise and draw me into their games. But not for long. Almost immediately I sense the difference between their perception of me and my own—and I much prefer my own. Once I see myself through my own eyes, it doesn't matter how anyone else looks at me. I don't have to live up to their vision. They don't have to like my feelings. I don't have to play their game. I may get hurt when I give my feelings their freedom, but I also get a lot of satisfaction out of life. Besides, getting hurt isn't the end of everything; there *is* such a thing as recovery.

Many ACOAs have memory gaps, some of them huge, when they try to recall their childhood. Some of us say we didn't have a childhood, but that isn't quite what happened. We had a childhood that is too painful for us to remember, so we block it out. I don't advise anyone with such a history of pain to go back over it alone. Go with your adult. Let this mature, dependable part of yourself look at your past and reinterpret what happened there. Let it fill in the gaps, correct the distortions, clean out the lies, and give you an honest memory.

Letting Go of Control

"I try to control myself now, but not other people," Sara says. A typical ACOA, she took responsibility for other people's lives by trying to control them. "I had to keep something wrong from happening, and if it happened anyway, I had to fix it.

"For instance, I taught my kids to do their own laundry since they were old enough to reach the dials on the laundry machines. But I was such a fusspot about *how* they did it. Everything had to look just so, or I'd be on their backs to do it over. My husband helps me with our laundry. I know he doesn't like doing it, but he knows it's fair because I work, too. But we'd be folding a big pile of sheets and towels and I'd be telling him he wasn't folding them the right way.

"You know how kids are about their rooms? Well, I didn't like myself for doing it, but I'd look in their rooms while they were out and when I saw what a mess they were in, I'd get mad! As soon as they came home I'd tell them to clean up the mess, and then *they'd* be mad because I violated their privacy.

"I even used to act as an interpreter for my husband when we were with our friends. He's very free and easy with people, and sometimes he'll say something outrageous, but I'd feel so embarrassed that I'd think, *What must they think of him?* and I'd butt right in and say, 'What John really means is . . .'

"If you were to look in my closet, you'd see my clothes organized into skirts here, blouses there, shoes over there. All the hangers would be facing the same way. If you wanted to borrow a scarf, I could tell you, 'Go to the chest next to the window, the third drawer down, and in the left-hand corner you'll find a pile of scarves.'

"That's all okay, if that's how I want to keep *my* things. But it's not okay for me to want everybody else to be the same way. And one day I began to realize that. *You dummy!* I said to myself, *Why do you have to louse everything up?*

"Did my kids' laundry really have to be spotless? Wasn't it more important for them to learn how to look after their own things? Because *I* certainly didn't have time to do it! And why did I have to go and look in their rooms? I knew they'd be a mess, so why did I have to look and get angry? *Leave the door closed,* I told myself, *then you'll be happy!*

"One night my husband and I were standing across from each other, folding a sheet, and he started to fold it his way, and I was about to say, 'No, do it *this* way,' but I stopped. I thought, *This man doesn't want to stand here folding sheets any more than I do. Does it really matter how he folds them? If I don't allow him the freedom to do it his way, he's not going to do it.* So I kept my mouth shut. Now I don't give a damn how the laundry gets folded. I just want to get it done."

Sara also stopped editing her husband's remarks. "It's not up to me to control what people think of him. That's his business—and theirs. At some point I realized that if something didn't come from my lips, I didn't have to apologize for it. If it *did* come from my lips, then it was mine to deal with.

"Once that kind of a realization comes along, then, damn it! we have to do something with it. We have to try it out and see what happens. We have to make a change in the way we live by putting that realization to work for us.

"Look at it this way—if you're going to do some fixing, then fix yourself. Let go of other people's lives.

Maybe you'll have to do a little damage control now and then to protect yourself, but don't do more than that."

Taking Care of Ourselves

Ellen is a guidance counselor at a regional high school and she's accustomed to young people stopping by her office and saying, "Got a minute?" Until recently she always said yes. "Sometimes I didn't have a minute, but I'd say yes anyway. It got so I hardly ever ate lunch, and I never scheduled time between appointments so I could have a moment to clear my head before I plunged into another problem."

Ellen, the child of an alcoholic mother, has a long history of ignoring her own needs. She remembers the day she first saw her mother drunk. It was during World War II, when Ellen was in grade school, and two days after her father was drafted into the army. "I blamed it on the war," she says. "I thought my mother started drinking because she was worried about my father and because she was afraid to be alone, but now I think that the reasons why she drank must have been there all along. But I felt it was my job to look after her. I always came straight home from school because I was worried about her, and I'd find her on the living-room sofa, crying and saying all kinds of crazy things. I'd help her up to her bedroom and put her to bed, but two minutes later she'd be downstairs again, looking for a drink. I used to be afraid somebody would walk in and see her that way."

When Ellen got married, she worked hard at being a good wife and mother. "I thought that was all I needed," she says. Then, when her children were grown, she came face-to-face with something entirely new: her own needs. "I realized I still had some years ahead of me and I started to think about what I wanted to do with them." Ellen decided to go back to school. "I wasn't sure what I wanted to do, but my education was out of date." To her surprise, her husband objected. She could bring her education up to date, he said, but he didn't want his wife working. "He wanted me there when he came home, and he couldn't understand why I wanted to do anything else. He kept saying, 'We don't need the money!'"

By that time, Ellen had become aware that growing up with an alcoholic parent had left its mark on her. "When I looked back over my life, I felt very resentful about all the giving I had done, without ever getting anything back. But there wasn't anybody I could blame, because I was the one who wanted to do the giving. I mean, if you keep offering things to people, how can you blame them for taking them?

"When my husband told me he didn't want me to work, I almost changed my mind about going back to school, out of habit. But something in me said, 'If you don't stand up for what you want now, you'll never do it.' That was very hard for me to do, because I had never disagreed with my husband about anything, and he was used to getting his own way. I even considered the possibility that I might lose him if I didn't give in, and I don't know what I would have done if that had happened."

Ellen's relationship with her husband is quite different from what it used to be. "In some ways it's difficult," she says, "but it's better!" When she explained how she felt about doing something useful with the rest of her life—when he understood that it was as important to her as his career was to him—his attitude changed. It wasn't easy for him to give up the convenience of a wife who lived only for him. He grumbled about taking his shirts to the laundry and doing the dinner dishes because Ellen had to do homework. "But I think he enjoys my company much more now," Ellen says.

To Ellen's dismay, however, her newfound independence did not spill over into her job. "I almost burned out after one year," she recalls. "I wasn't just trying to help students decide where they wanted to go to college—I was trying to solve *all* their problems! I was responsible for everybody but myself."

Ellen's feelings were very familiar to me. When I look back now at the way I used to think when I felt responsible for making my parents happy, I realize that I had everything backward. I thought that if I looked after them, they would be able to look after me. But that isn't true. The only way I can look after anybody is to look after myself first. I can't ask anyone else to fulfill my needs; I have to fulfill them myself. That's what growing up is all about.

Now, when a student asks Ellen, "Got a minute?" she stops and asks herself, *Do I?* "And if I do have a minute," she says, "is it a minute I need for myself? I don't give up my lunchtime anymore. If a student stops by just when I'm going to lunch, I'll say, 'I'd like to see you, but let's schedule an appointment for sometime this afternoon. I'm going to lunch now.' And guess what? The world keeps on turning!"

CHAPTER FOUR

ENDING THE LONELINESS

LIKE ANYONE ELSE, ACOAs have friends. We have lovers, we have spouses, we have children and grandchildren. We have neighbors, co-workers, and business associates. But something is missing from our relationships—emotional accessibility. We don't let people get close to us, and we're afraid to get close to them. We know too well what can happen.

Steve would like to forget what happened the summer he was twelve. "That's when I let my guard down," he says.

Steve's best friend, Pat, lived two blocks away. The two boys were in the same class and had been friends ever since they could remember. Pat swung by Steve's house every weekday morning and they biked to school together. After school they shot hoops in Pat's driveway or roughhoused on the ballfield until dinnertime. "In all that time, I don't think Pat got a chance to say more than ten words to my parents," Steve says. "Sounds peculiar, doesn't it? But I arranged it that way. I always made sure I was waiting outside when Pat came by. If he showed up when I didn't expect him, I got him out of the house so fast he couldn't tell what was going on. After school I never said, 'Let's go to my house.' I'd wait for him to say it.

"I never told Pat about my mother and father drinking. I made up stories about them so they'd seem normal. A few times Pat's mother would say something like, 'We'd like to meet your family, Steve, maybe they'd like to come over for dinner sometime,' and I'd say, 'Sure,' figuring she'd forget it.

"Pat was a good guy, and his family was very nice to me. On holidays I'd spend all day at their house because I sure as hell didn't want to be in my place. But I knew them better than they knew me.

"Then, that summer I was twelve, my mother said, 'Why don't you ask Pat to come to the beach house for a few days?' We had this little place at the shore where we'd go for a few weeks every summer, and rent it out the rest of the season. I used to dread those weeks because my mother and father would be drunk from beginning to end. All their friends would come and stay over, and it was always one big bash. I hated it. I used to get out early in the morning and stay on the beach all day with my friends. I'd sneak home to change my clothes and I'd stay out late. Sometimes I'd get lucky and one of my friends would ask me to sleep over at his house so I wouldn't have to go home until the next morning. My folks used to look forward to those weeks all year. It was their vacation, and when it was over they couldn't remember any of it.

"I blame myself for what happened because I knew better. But I thought, *Maybe if Pat's there, they'll do things right.* Besides, I liked the idea of showing Pat around and introducing him to my friends. So I said yes, and Pat said sure, he'd like to come, and his parents said okay, he could. His mother even spoke on the phone to my mother about it, and my mother handled it perfectly. She agreed it would be nice if the two families got together sometime and maybe they could do that after we all came back from the beach. She even had me thinking we might start to be like any other family.

"We were at the beach for two weeks before Pat came, and nothing was changing. So I started plan-

ning how I could keep Pat away from the house as
much as possible. For two days that worked, although
it was harder to find ways to feed the two of us instead
of just me. And he was starting to ask questions about
the other people who were staying at our house. He
could see there was a lot of drinking going on, but I
kept telling myself he wouldn't put two and two
together.

"Then, on the third day he was there, his parents
drove up. Pat and I came back to the house to change
into dry suits and there they were sitting on the front
porch, sober as judges, and everybody else as drunk as
skunks. They took my folks by surprise all right, and I
could see what was going on. Pat's parents just wanted
to see what kind of people their kid was staying with.
I'd want to know the same thing about my kid's friends
today, but back then I thought it was a shitty thing to
do. My whole cover was blown. There was my mother
playing the *grande dame*, which she always did when
she was drunk, and spilling clam dip all over their
laps. My father was up to his usual tricks, trying to
get somebody to disagree with him so he could tell
him off and throw him out.

"It was a long evening, and when Pat's family left,
they took Pat with them. They were nice about it.
They just said one of Pat's uncles was coming to visit
and that he counted on seeing Pat, so it was best if he
went home with them.

"I remember helping Pat get his things together
and knowing that we weren't going to be friends anymore. Actually I hated him for finding out about me. I
was so ashamed."

The friendship did end.

"Pat and I still biked to school together, and we'd
shoot hoops in his driveway, but it wasn't the same. I
was uncomfortable with him because I thought now
that he knew what my mother and father were like,

he'd probably think there was something wrong with me, too. I started making excuses and hanging out somewhere else. And boy, after that, did I ever keep everybody at a distance!"

Steve knows now that, even at its best, his relationship with Pat wasn't close. "I never let him get to know me well because I thought he wouldn't want to be my friend. I was that way with everybody."

Why We Don't Get Close

It's not surprising that children who grow up in alcoholic families become loners. First of all, we really aren't sure who we are, and, second, we think we aren't very nice. We ask ourselves, constantly, the question we're certain is on everyone else's mind: How could anything good come out of the insanity that was our home life?

In school, we don't want our friends to know that our parents drink, so we don't tell them. But when you have to keep a lot of things to yourself, there's nothing left to share. You can't tell someone how you feel because some of your feelings are pretty ugly. You can't tell someone what you did last night, because last night your father fell down drunk on the kitchen floor and you and your sister had to help your mother get him into bed.

Sara says she's still emotionally reserved with her friends. "Sometimes my friends will express feelings toward me that, although I have feelings toward them, their feelings seem stronger than mine."

Marian, like Paul, can open up only to other ACOAs. "I don't think anyone else can understand me," she says.

Fran says she has to be careful about her friendships. "I tend to let people take advantage of me."

Martin says, "Don't get me wrong. I like people. I'm just not comfortable with them."

Doug says he's too busy to get to know people. He works long hours and coaches a high-school swim team.

Almost all of us can remember a few special teachers in our childhood who went out of their way to know us better. But we couldn't respond because there were so many things we couldn't say, and we were afraid we'd let something slip.

It's very hard being a child and not being able to talk about your parents, because there isn't much else going on in your life at that early age. Although you were ashamed of your parents, you desperately wanted their love, so you didn't want to say anything bad about them. In fact, you covered up for them. You told people only the good things and left out everything else. You exaggerated a little, you told your teachers how much your parents loved you and how much they sacrificed for you. But you didn't tell them about the bars, and the fights, and the drinking, and getting sick, and the money that wasn't there—because if your teachers knew the truth about your parents, maybe they wouldn't want to waste their time on you. And if you *told* them that your parents drank, they'd say, "What kind of a kid are you to say things like that about your parents?"

You couldn't talk to your parents' friends, either. Some of them could be real charmers, and you'd want to confide in them. You'd start to tell them how frightened you were when your mother and father didn't come home all night, and how you thought maybe they had an accident. You'd ask what you could do when they started arguing with each other. That was about as far as you got before your charming confidant began to tell you what your parents had already told you many times before: You were an ungrateful, spoiled little liar! Then there were the others, the ones who got that anxious look in their eyes and changed the subject. Or the ones who gave you a quick hug and told you not to worry, everything was going to be just fine.

Sometimes you felt as if you could talk to a friend's parents. They were always glad to see you and they said you were one of the family. But the minute you mentioned *your* family, they asked too many questions.

The child of an alcoholic parent isn't imagining things when he says there wasn't anyone he could talk to. There wasn't. Least of all could he approach his parents. Talking to the alcoholic about the effects of his behavior is like throwing a gasoline bomb into a volcano. Years later, when the now-grown child is diagnosed as withdrawn, reclusive, aloof, and distant, he nods his head in agreement. He remembers when he wanted to be close to people, he remembers wanting to share what was going on inside him. But he remembers that it never seemed to be possible. And, in his loneliness, he wonders how anybody is ever able to pull it off.

Perfection or Nothing

If there is such a thing as normal, I fit the description when I was growing up. I made friends easily. I was comfortable with adults. I was a follower in some areas, and in others I led. I could compete as well as be a spectator. Winning didn't distract me, nor did losing destroy me. I appeared to be quite well-balanced —to the degree that some of my flakier friends' parents pointed to me as a good example. They didn't know—but I knew—that I was a phony. I was the wrong little kid trying to be the perfect adult.

I never felt I was being honest with people, and the

more I cared about someone, the more dishonest I felt. To my knowledge, I never pretended to be more than I was. I pretended to be less. I would do anything for a friend—except let her know what I thought, felt, wanted, or was. I could be dying inside, and no one could tell. I could be ready to burst with happiness, and I kept it to myself. I never talked about my family or where I grew up. If someone asked me whether my parents were living, I said yes and didn't elaborate.

I was, of course, very busy trying to read the people I cared about so that I could respond to what *they* thought, felt, wanted, and were. I didn't lie about myself; I simply tried to make myself become whatever someone I liked wanted me to be—and that's why I never felt genuine. I wasn't trying to deceive; I was trying to invent myself.

The person I invented—and I invented myself many times over, depending upon whom I wanted to please— had to be perfect at whatever she tried to do. That's the way an ACOA tries to make up for all the deficiencies she thinks she has: She'll be the best at whatever she's called upon to be, and maybe no one will notice how inferior she really is. It's a goal she can't ever achieve, at least not for long, but no matter how many times she fails, she keeps trying again. She doesn't understand that no one is perfect; she thinks everybody else is.

It shocks me a little now to remember what anxious, negative feelings I used to have whenever I met someone I wanted to know better. The thoughts that typically went through my mind were a rapid-fire syncopation of admiration for the other person and a putdown of myself:

Oh, what a fascinating person she is!
I must seem terribly dull to her.
She seems so sure of herself.

I feel so clumsy.
What a mind!
I can't think of anything intelligent to say.
She's got a great sense of humor.
I'll laugh at just the right moment. I know how to
   do that. But I'd better not say anything funny
   because maybe she'll think I'm competing with
   her.
*She comes right out and says what she thinks. I like
   that. And I like the way she does it, without being
   nasty.*
I have to be careful, though. I wouldn't want to say
   something and then find out she doesn't agree
   with me.

All this mental frenzy occurred within a fraction of
a second and kept on for as long as I was in the other
person's presence. I honestly don't know how I made
it through a day, but I suspect that my fear of being
rejected—like my childhood fear of being abandoned—
was a source of energy in itself. I was convinced that if
I wasn't perfect, I was nothing.

Usually the other person had no idea what was
going on inside me, but very often my inability to
relax and be open about myself made it impossible for
us to begin a relationship. Or I thought I was so
inferior that I couldn't possibly measure up to the
other person's expectations, and didn't wait around to
be rejected. Sometimes, however, my desperate efforts
to be perfect were very appealing to people who, like
my alcoholic parents, needed a player for their games.
Either way, I lost, so you can understand why relationships were so difficult for me.

But—that was the way I lived when I was pretending
to be an adult and knowing all the while that I was a
frightened child. Becoming an adult makes a difference:
It ends the loneliness and makes recovery possible.

There's an Easier Way

It is natural for a child to seek the hand of someone stronger and wiser than himself, someone who can guide him through the world and protect him from its dangers. And it is natural for an adult to respond to those needs. When the ACOA's natural child and natural adult begin to make contact with each other, a loving relationship naturally follows. This is the beginning of our recovery, because from that moment on, the wounds of the past can begin to heal.

"When you first begin to separate into a child and an adult, you have an intellectual understanding of each other," says Dr. Geraldine DePaula. "You're just becoming aware of each other's existence. But as you begin to come together, you reach an emotional understanding of each other. This happens on an *affective* level of your life. It affects every level of your being— what you think, what you feel, what you do, what you are. This is very important, because it's on this affective level that the healing of the child's wounds actually occurs. We all can understand things intellectually, but only when we move beyond that and begin to understand things in our heart do we begin to heal."

There will always be times when old habits and responses unexpectedly intrude, and we will find ourselves behaving in the same old way. But we will notice the difference immediately and be able to do something about it. The adult will see that the child is taking on something he can't handle and will lovingly move him aside. Relieved, the child will wait patiently while the adult deals with the situation.

"When the adult in us has an affective understanding of the child, the adult is concerned with how the child feels and how the child can grow," Dr. DePaula says. "And when a person becomes aware that the anxiety she feels is actually the anxiety of the child, then the adult in her can do something about it. Maybe not right away—we may have to postpone addressing the child's needs long enough to function more effectively as an adult in a certain situation. But we know we can trust ourselves to take care of the child as soon as possible.

"By then, the child in us has learned that, 'Yes, I will be attended to. I will have my hearing.' So the child can wait. The child *can't* wait if she never really gets attended to. Then she becomes most demanding. The children who are not paid attention to when they have needs are the ones who become the pests. If you watch little kids, you know who gets listened to."

I don't try to hide anymore, because I know I'm not a terrible person. I'm not perfect, either. But the adult and the child in me have a pretty good relationship. We let each other know how we feel. If we agree, that's fine. If we don't, that's okay, too. We don't try to change each other, but we do try to find out what makes each other tick, because we'd like to help each other tick better.

When it comes to rejection, the child in me still doesn't like it. But, then, who does? At least I'm not afraid of it. The adult in me has taught me three important things about it:

- It's a normal part of life, not the whole of it.
- It doesn't always happen.
- If it does, I can survive it.

As for feelings, I know I have them. But it's important for other people to know I have them, too. How else are they going to know who I am?

The hard part about being myself was getting started. I had pretended to be so many different people for so long that I didn't know how to begin to be me. My adult suggested, "Why not begin there? Let people know you're not sure of yourself."

"But that's not a good feeling," my anxious child said.

"Maybe not, but it's honest," my adult replied.

So I did. (By then my child was beginning to trust my adult to protect her, no matter what happened.) If I had to speak to someone about a touchy matter, I began by admitting I was uncomfortable. Somehow that made it easier for me to talk to people. If I couldn't do anything to help a friend with a big problem, I told him how helpless I felt—then I could tell him how much I cared.

My adult also helped me to be more honest with myself. For instance, taking off and landing in a plane made my child anxious, but did she show it? You bet she didn't! She actually thought it was her responsibility to help other people deal with their fears by concealing hers.

"Baloney!" my adult said. "There's nothing you can do to help them—help yourself. Close your eyes, hold on to me, say a prayer!" She was right—it's much easier for me to take off and land now because I'm not trying to look as if it doesn't affect me. And if someone asks me if I'm afraid, I answer, "Yes, very!"—speaking for my child. You'd be surprised how many people agree with me, and how much more comfortable it is for us to share our anxieties.

Before speaking in public, my child was always afraid she was going to say something dumb. At times my throat got so dry I could hardly say a word. Then one day while I was waiting to do a live radio interview, my adult said, "Suppose you do say something stupid? These are nice people—they'll forgive you!" That gave me the courage to tell my interviewer that I was nervous. "So am I," he said. "Some of us never get

over it. Here, drink some water—in little sips. It helps."
I don't know whether it was the water that helped or
the fact that the interviewer and I were already engaged in easy conversation by the time the program
started, but I had such a good time, I forgot I was
nervous.

It used to be hard for me to ask for help. I claimed I
was trying to prove I could take care of myself, but
that wasn't true. I couldn't ask for help because I was
sure I'd be turned down. "That's always a possibility,"
my adult said. "But you can always ask someone else.
In fact, why not give people a choice? When you ask
for help—tell them to feel free to say no." I did, and it
made the asking easier.

My adult knew what she was talking about. Being
honest, not only with other people but with myself,
was like opening up a logjam. Feelings that had piled
on top of each other began to come out, and the relief
was so great that I knew I would never again be able
to hold them back. The nagging sense that I wasn't
genuine began to leave, and in its place was the beginning of what I can only describe as *okayness*. I
could tell I was making progress when a friend said,
"You're such an open person—I really like knowing
how you feel." I hadn't always been that way, but she
didn't remember and that was fine with me.

A more tangible proof of my emotional accessibility
came one spring day when I was driving along a
back-country road and was stopped for speeding. It
was my fault. The weather was beautiful, the music
on my radio was exciting, and I wasn't paying attention to the posted speed limits as they changed from
45 to 35, but at the sight of the police car's flashing
lights in my rearview mirror, I was terrified. Only
once before in all my life had I been cited for speeding,
and I was overcome with guilt—not ACOA-style guilt,
but the real thing!

When the police officer asked for my license and registration, I pulled out my wallet so quickly that its contents slithered into my lap, and as I fumbled among bills and credit cards I knocked most of them onto the floor. I started to apologize, then realized that wasn't how I felt.

"I'm scared to death!" I told the officer.

He was stern, but without softening his expression he said, "Take your time. It's normal to be nervous."

My heart was still beating like a ladle on an old pot, but I felt a little better. I didn't have to pretend to be cool. It was okay to be scared. It was okay to admit I did something wrong and to pay the price for it, but not one emotional cent more. The citation was expensive, and I've been more attentive to speed signs ever since, but I drove off with a valuable realization: I had nothing to hide—from anyone. It was okay to be me.

CHAPTER FIVE

GETTING THE LOVE
WE NEED

'TWAS THE NIGHT *after* Christmas, and you never saw a more depressed group. They were ACOAs straggling into a church basement for a weekly meeting sponsored by a local Al-Anon chapter. Usually most of the group showed up early and waited restlessly for the meeting to begin, and begin it did on the dot of seven. But not on this night. It was 7:15 and only eight people were present. Average attendance was about fifteen, but you could hear slow, reluctant footsteps in the hall outside and you knew they would stop at this room.

By 7:30 there were twenty-two men and women crowded around two large tables pushed together, far too many for a good give-and-take. But this was not a night to split the group in two; you could *feel* the need to be there, and maybe the numbers helped. Veteran members knew exactly what was going on. "It's the holidays," one of them said. "It's always this way around the holidays."

Some of the newcomers nodded and smiled self-consciously. Now they understood. "Not that it helps," one said.

A slim, attractive, thirtyish woman volunteered to lead the group in discussion. "I miss being with my family," she said, as a way of getting started.

"I thought you had a family," said an elfin-faced woman across the table. "Don't you?"

"I'm not talking about my husband and daughters," the first woman said, a bit snappishly. "I mean my parents. My mother and father. I miss being with them for the holidays." Her voice broke and she bent her head. "I'm sorry!" she murmured. "I swore I wouldn't cry!"

The woman sitting next to her passed a tissue. "It's okay to cry," she said comfortingly. "It's good to cry."

"No, it's isn't!" the first woman said. Now she was angry and she looked around the table accusingly. "You're always trying to get me to cry, but I'm not going to!"

"That's okay, too, Karen," a heavyset man in a thick sweater said evenly. "Nobody's telling you what to do."

"I know," Karen said apologetically. "It's just a bad night for me, that's all. If I didn't have this place to come to, I don't know what I would have done. My husband thinks I'm crazy, and I know I spoiled his Christmas. Everything was so nice, so good. We had this big dinner and the tree, and everybody was having such a great time—except me. I was miserable. I'm that way every year at Christmas."

"We all are," someone said.

"Yeah, but I'll bet you something," the man in the big sweater said, leaning forward and resting his arms on the table. "I'll bet every one of you always had a lousy Christmas when you were a kid." He smiled, seeing the others nod. "We all did. But we forget that. We start telling ourselves it wasn't that bad. We start falling back into the same old lies and cover stories about how great it was to be with good old Mom and Dad at Christmas.

"Well, just to jog your memory a little, I'll tell you what I remember. Christmas was hell! I'd hold my breath all day long, wondering what my father was going to do this year. Was he going to throw the tree through the window? Cut himself trying to slice the turkey because he was so drunk he couldn't tell the bird from his hand? Burn up our presents in the fireplace? We could always count on him for something. We used to spend days fixing the house up for the holidays, and he'd ruin it every year. It was almost as if he enjoyed it.

"Remember? Sure, you do. You probably have better memories than mine." He looked around the table, inviting comment, but no one took him up on it. Disappointed, he leaned back in his chair and let his hands rest in his lap. "It doesn't matter, does it?" he said sadly. "Even if we remember what it was like, we still want to go back. I'd go if I could—but my father's dead."

One by one they began to share some of their memories, all of them grim. By the end of the evening, they reached a conclusion. "We have to remember that alcoholism is a disease," Karen said, attempting to summarize for the others. "Our parents did the best they could, and in their own way they loved us." No one disagreed.

The meeting ended and some of the members stood around in small groups, recalling the past in more detail. Gradually they all left. No one said, "Happy New Year."

We Want to Believe

Two women I know were concerned about a troubled family in their church congregation. The mother was alcoholic and didn't seem capable of looking after her two young children, and the father was often away for long periods of time. One woman speculated that the children might be better off in a foster home, but the other woman disagreed. "No, no," she said, "alcoholics can be very loving people."

It's a popular misconception, and most children of alcoholic parents subscribe to it. We remember so many mornings after when our alcoholic parents suffered such intense pain that we couldn't stand it. We'd tell them that they really hadn't behaved so badly because we didn't want to add to their misery. Ask us if our parents loved us and we will search our memories feverishly for examples to prove it. But somewhere in the telling we begin to realize there was something wrong with the kind of love we got. "My father used to lavish me with presents," Fran says. "He didn't have the money to buy me things, but he worked on a big farm and he used to say I could have any dog or cat or horse I wanted." Then the smile fades as Fran remembers that her father used to break a lot of his promises.

Steve remembers that "whenever I needed money, my father would always help me out." Then he'd add that "Money was the only thing my father could ever give me—and he made me sweat for it!"

Sara says her father "was a very affectionate man. He never left the house without kissing my mother, and he'd always kiss us good night when we went up to bed." She'll tell you how she used to sit and talk to him after dinner. "If I had a problem, I could always go to him for advice—until he started drinking more. That's when I lost a father. There wasn't any point in talking to him because the next day he couldn't remember what we said."

Elizabeth's father used to brag about her to his friends. "He'd call me in to sit on his lap and he'd say all kinds of wonderful things about me." Finally it dawned on Elizabeth that "he never said anything nice to me when his friends weren't around."

Doug's father lived with him for the last two years of his life. "We got along pretty well and I actually enjoyed his company," Doug says. But he qualifies that memory: "He lived on the same property, but in a trailer by himself. He cooked his own meals and we only saw each other now and then. Besides, he didn't have anybody else in the world, so he had to behave himself. He depended on me for everything."

It doesn't help an ACOA to tell him that his alcoholic parent loved him as well as he could. He's been saying that to himself all his life, and he still doesn't know what love is. He thinks it means someone needs him, because that's the only way his parent could love him.

What the Alcoholic Parent Needs

"There are two kinds of love, universal and unconditional," explains Dr. Yvonne Kaye, a Philadelphia-area psychologist who works extensively with ACOAs. "Universal love is loving humanity itself, and not going out of your way to hurt people. Unconditional love is loving someone without any expectation of a return—*and loving yourself first.* You can't love anyone unless you love yourself, because that's the way you learn *how* to love."

The child of an alcoholic parent is brought up to love the parent first, and never gets around to loving herself. She expects the parent to do that. Consequently she never really learns how to love at all, but she assumes that other people do. She sees love as something she has to work very hard to earn, yet it can be taken away or withheld at the parent's whim. She learns how to give but not how to get, and she expects the parent to make up for that discrepancy, too. When the parent doesn't, or can't, give the child what she needs, the child persuades herself that she didn't need anything, anyway, so she can continue to believe the parent loves her. She will deny anything to prove that point. If she is at all aware that she gets nothing in return for all her hard work, she deals with her disappointment by saying, "That's the way love is." She will repeatedly prove how right she is by seeking out people who have no love to give.

The alcoholic parent cannot possibly return the child's love because she doesn't love herself. She cannot fulfill a child's emotional needs because she herself is a bundle of needs that demands attention. The alcoholic sees herself not only as a victim of life's misfortunes, but the greatest victim of all, and she will tolerate no competition. In her eyes, everyone else in the world gets a break—except the alcoholic. Everyone else succeeds, enjoys life, is treated with kindness and respect, is loved without hesitation, is more beautiful, healthier, richer, and certainly happier than the alcoholic. While other people can solve their problems, the alcoholic's are monumental and everlasting, and no one is more deserving of pity and sacrifice. She is so bereft of self-love that she doesn't recognize love when it is offered to her and usually will insist on more than anyone can give.

Trying to satisfy an alcoholic parent's needs is like walking across an emotional minefield. What looks like safe ground may blow up in your face if you:

• Express needs of your own
• Achieve something of your own
• Pay attention to someone else's needs

When Sara told her parents she was pregnant, her father wasn't interested in her struggle to decide whether to marry the child's father, have the baby out of wedlock, or abort it. "He didn't say anything at first," she remembers. "Then he said, 'This means you're not going to be the first one in our family to finish college,' and walked out. Nice!"

Roy's father always pushed him to excel in sports. When Roy pitched a no-hitter in a high-school baseball game, his father picked a fight with him and called him a "cocky bastard." The fight became so violent that Roy left home at the age of sixteen.

Betsy's first child, a daughter, is three years old and her mother has seen the child only once. "She doesn't live that far away, but she always finds some reason not to come and see us. When things didn't work out well for me, she was always there, but now that I'm happy and have a good marriage and a beautiful baby, I never see my mother."

Steve thought his parents expected him to go to college. "They always talked that way, and money wasn't a problem. But when I started applying to different schools, they told me not to set my sights too high. 'Try for the easier schools,' they said, 'because you're not the smartest kid in the world.' Then, when I got accepted by some pretty good schools, they said maybe they couldn't afford to send me to college at all. I didn't know what to think. I felt as if I did something wrong, but I didn't know what. Finally, at the last minute, they said I could go to college, but by then I was sure I wasn't good enough."

The only word I ever misspelled as a child was *egg*. I once spelled it *eeg* on a test, and my parents never let me forget it. Whenever I brought home a good report card or received an honor of any kind, my mother and stepfather acknowledged it by teasing me about *eeg*, and never with a word of praise. For years after I was old enough to work, they never asked what I did for a living. I never talked about my career because I knew they would find a way to belittle it, and my ego wasn't strong enough to withstand that. Even now my stepfather expresses surprise when he asks what I did today and I tell him I was working. My books are on a table in a corner of his dining room, but he hasn't read them. Neither did my mother. If, to keep up appearances, they glanced at something I wrote, they always dismissed it by saying they didn't understand it.

Eventually, the child of an alcoholic does whatever she thinks will please the parent, and tries not to do anything else. But that isn't always possible because the needs of the alcoholic parent often contradict each other. Your alcoholic parent may want you to fail because that makes her feel superior to you—but if you fail, you may call on her for help, and she can't handle that. Or she may want you to succeed because it makes her look good—but it also threatens her view of herself as a tragic victim, because if you can do something about your life, then why can't she? She may criticize you for not being popular, but if you bring home a few friends, she'll find fault with them. She'll badmouth your favorite man and give rave reviews to the one you can't stand. You may think she doesn't want you around, but just try to break away from her and you'll find out how strong your bonds are.

Loving the Self First

As long as we think that love means someone needs us, we'll never know love. We'll know only frustration, self-sacrifice, self-blame, self-contempt, pain, and confusion about our identity. As long as we expect the people we love to make us happy because we try so hard to make them happy, we will never know love. We'll know disappointment and resentment. Why do people use us so badly?

Because we let them. We give them what we need for ourselves, and we expect them to give us what they don't have.

"When I was married to my first husband," Elizabeth says, "I never did anything for myself. I was a slave to my husband and children because I thought I was supposed to be a slave. But I expected something in return—I expected to feel good about myself. I didn't.

"In my second marriage I was the exact opposite. Instead of being the submissive little wife, I took control of everything. My husband had been married and divorced, too, and he had a son by his first marriage. When the boy said he wanted to live with us, I decided he could. I decided where we would live, what kind of house we would have, and how much we could pay for it. I didn't believe two people could argue as much as we did, because I wanted everything my way. Now that doesn't mean I did something for myself, because I didn't. 'My way' meant doing what I thought would make everyone happy—so I could feel good about myself. And, again, I didn't.

"Either way, I really didn't like the person I was. And I wasn't getting anything back from my relationships."

After Elizabeth's second marriage ended in divorce, she blamed herself for the failure. "I was starting on the old guilt trip again," she says. "Then I realized I didn't have to do that. I was brought up to believe that suffering makes you a better person, so whenever I suffered from guilt or anything else, I'd console myself by saying I'd be better off for it. But all of a sudden I realized that was bullshit! *Why* did I have to suffer? Couldn't I enjoy life and *still* be a good person?

"I had had a lot of therapy by then, and finally it began to change the way I looked at myself. I saw that all the time I was knocking myself out trying to make everybody happy, I was ignoring a very unhappy little girl inside of me."

Children of alcoholics, like any other children, cannot love until we are loved. And we cannot get that love from our parents because they have none to give. We have to get it from—and give it to—ourselves. It has to grow out of a loving relationship between the child and the adult in us—the child looking to the adult for affirmation that she's an okay person, and the adult feeling good about herself because she is taking care of the child. This is how self-esteem begins.

"What a relief it was for me to realize that I could look after this little girl," Elizabeth says. "Sometimes, when I fall into old habits, my adult picks up on it. She'll say to the child, 'Look, you don't have to do those things anymore. There's a better way to live—I'll show you.'

"I think the biggest difference came about in my relationship with my children. They're grown now, and I feel as if they're my friends. But sometimes when they call me, I can tell, without their saying it, that something is wrong. Maybe it's just the way their voice sounds, or the long silences. I used to annoy the hell out of them by asking, 'What's the matter?' because I wanted to help them with whatever was bothering them. And if they told me, I'd come up with one solution after another.

"I stopped doing that because I realized that I didn't want anyone doing it to me. When I have a problem, my adult knows how to listen, and I like that. Sometimes I'm not looking for a solution, I just want someone to get close enough to share my feelings. To listen, that's all. I think that's what my children want at this stage of their lives. So I listen, and if there's a long silence, I just let it be. But my children know I'm here, and if they want my help, they know it's here. I'm learning how to let them be—because that's what I'm learning to do with myself. It makes me feel loved when someone can do that, and it's what I think my children are beginning to feel from me."

Sara says she learned about unconditional love from her dog. "He doesn't care what I do or don't do, or if I make the biggest goof in the world. He wags his tail when he sees me and comes running. He's happy just because I'm here. I'm starting to be that way about myself—to feel good about myself, not for any particular reason, but just because I'm here."

Breaking the Pattern

When you exist only to make someone else happy—because you want that person or persons to make *you* happy—your life is always precarious. What will happen if you fail?

When you devote all your energy to taking care of someone else's needs—because you assume that your needs will be taken care of in return—you live with anxiety. Will you have enough to give?

When you depend on someone else to define you—because you want an identity—you feel dishonest. Suppose someone finds out who you really are?

My first attempts at loving myself were very clumsy. In fact, I was trying to satisfy a friend who was concerned about my lack of self-esteem, and I wanted to please her. Later I wanted to please my husband in the same way because he said I didn't think enough of myself. To me, these observations seemed like expressions of concern from people who would *love me if* . . . And since I was familiar with the promise to *love me if* . . . , I plunged right in and tried to make myself feel loved. Of course, I knew I wasn't. There were too many things wrong with me. But I thought that loving myself meant giving myself one big emotional hug, and then everything would be all right.

The one big emotional hug accomplished absolutely nothing—except an uncomfortable feeling that I was putting myself on. But I went through the motions and both my friend and later my husband seemed to be pleased. Eventually, when I really did begin to love myself, I lost both the friend and the husband because I began to change in ways that didn't please them. I began to put my own needs before theirs, and that wasn't what they meant by loving myself.

A lot of people talk about loving the self without really knowing what it means. It's more than words. It's more than telling yourself you're a nice person who deserves a nice life. It's more than one big emotional hug. Loving yourself is a lasting relationship between the child in you and the adult in you. It gives you the tools you need to build your life: identity, caring, responsibility, and trust.

Identity means knowing who you are. This takes time, so don't try to hurry. You have to work your way out of old habits. For instance, you're accustomed to judging yourself according to other people's expectations and needs. If you had what they needed, you were okay. If you didn't, you were worthless.

Forget about judging. Think about learning. Be curious about yourself. Let your adult listen to your child. How does she respond to people, things, thoughts, behavior? What's important to her? How does she perceive the world? How does she want to live in it? How would she like to be treated? What does she hope to accomplish? Anything is acceptable. Nothing is impossible. Nothing is wrong. There are no virtues, no flaws. There is only the child you want to know. Learning who you are will take the rest of your life, but it can be a rewarding, fascinating education.

Caring means being sensitive to your feelings. If,

while you were growing up, your feelings weren't acceptable to your alcoholic parents, then your child suppressed them very quickly. But it was the suppression, not the feelings themselves, that made you uncomfortable. Now your adult can begin to intervene in that split-second moment between feeling and suppression. In the beginning, let your discomfort be a signal to your adult that your child is afraid and is covering up how she really feels about something. Don't force your child to reveal what she feels. You already know she's afraid, so deal with that first. Let her know you understand why she's afraid, and that it's all right. Then give her your protection. As she begins to feel safe and comforted, she'll realize that it's acceptable to be afraid. Eventually she will realize that your adult welcomes all her feelings. Gradually that moment between feeling and suppression will grow longer, until finally there is only the feeling and no suppression.

Responsibility means providing for your needs. With your child's help, you're learning who you are and how you feel. Now it's time for your adult to make some decisions. How can you use your abilities—both your strengths and limitations—to get what you want out of life? Never mind wondering what someone else wants—you've done enough of that. This time it's *your* needs that matter.

In the beginning, consider your needs one at a time. For instance, your child may love classical music and may wish she could be in the company of people who share that enjoyment. Your adult can act on those needs. You might decide to take a course in music appreciation, or learn to play an instrument, or join a music society. If your child is shy, consider subscribing to a series of concerts; sitting among the same other subscribers each time makes it easier to talk to someone. In time, your awareness of your needs will not only determine your goals, but how you go about attaining them.

Expect to feel selfish for a while. It's normal. You're accustomed to paying attention to everyone but yourself. When you begin to experience your own self-sufficiency, however, you'll be able to evaluate other people's demands more objectively. When you learn to treat yourself fairly, you'll know how to treat others fairly. Anything beyond that is unreasonable.

Trust means expressing who you are in everything you do. Loving ourselves is not all joy and celebration. Sometimes it results in a loss. If, by loving ourselves and meeting our own needs, we can no longer satisfy someone else's expectations, that person may not want to continue a relationship with us. And it may be a relationship we dearly wished to keep. Should that happen to you, don't ignore the importance of your disappointment. Pay attention to your feelings and allow yourself to grieve over your loss. Your child has been hurt and deserves to be comforted—and your adult knows how to do this. Yes, you can go on to other, healthier relationships, but don't rush into them. Allowing yourself to recover from your pain is part of loving yourself. And you will recover—because you will recognize it as something you need.

CHAPTER SIX

LETTING GO
OF A PARENT

AFTER YEARS OF A consuming relationship with my parents, I began to look for a way to end their hold over me. I was exhausted from trying to win their love and from living in a state of constant anxiety. It was time for me to think about my own life, my own future, my own problems.

When I was eighteen, I had to make an important decision: Should I get a job and move out on my own? Or should I go to college and endure four more years as a dependent in my parents' home? And a dependent I would be, because my parents made it clear that they would not pay for my room and board at school. I wanted to get out, but I knew I couldn't be independent for long without a better education. I "signed on" for four more years. I expected them to be a grueling test of my endurance, and they were.

I was never sure that my tuition would be paid at the beginning of each semester during my college years. My parents would always tell me that they couldn't afford to send me to school, and at the last minute they would relent and pay the bill. Those were the years before students could count on various forms of financial aid for their education. Scholarships and grants-in-aid were few and meager, and were awarded only on the basis of merit and financial need. To help pay my tuition I got a part-time job developing X rays for a dentist, and worked full time as a secretary every summer. Foolishly, I gave what I earned to my parents and put nothing aside for my expenses to and from school.

I lived at home in New Jersey and commuted to school in New York. I had never been given an allowance as a child. I was told to ask for what I needed, but when I saw what I had to go through to prove a need, I tried to need very little. Getting a hole in my shoe was my fault; growing out of my shoes was almost a crime; sickness, especially when it involved the cost of a doctor or medicine, was looked upon as deliberate meanness. Wanting something I could do without made me feel guilty and selfish.

Commuting to college, I couldn't do without carfare and lunch money, although on most days I brown-bagged it. But my parents still objected to a weekly allowance. Each morning I had to ask my mother for the exact amount of money I needed for the day, and every now and then she wanted an accounting of why I needed that amount. Sometimes I walked part of the way to school so I would have money for coffee with my friends, an extravagance I never admitted to my parents. And sometimes, when my parents were showing off to their drinking buddies, they became generous. I took the dollars they offered me and put them away to be spent judiciously on Christmas presents for them. After their nights of partying I searched the chairs and sofa crevices for coins that slipped out of pockets. With luck, I collected enough to get through a day without asking for carfare.

We were not a poor family: My stepfather was a salesman in a large corporation, and my mother was a secretary. Their combined income was above average in a time when most families got by on one salary. We enjoyed fringe benefits such as health insurance, bonuses, and a company car. We lived in an attractive apartment, and my parents dressed very well. But there was never money in the bank, never enough for a down payment on a house, and always a crisis at tuition time—and tuitions then were much lower than they are now. Our money went into drinking and the extravagant entertainment that often went along with it. Every Friday night we were rich; every Monday morning we were broke. Eventually I was able to qualify for a few small scholarships, which helped to ease my discomfort, but financial aid was out of the question because my parents earned too much money.

Money, or the lack of it, wasn't my only problem. I didn't realize, until I went to college, that it's very hard to concentrate in the home of an alcoholic. There's too much going on. If it's quiet, you know it won't last. If it's noisy, it will probably get worse. You can count on arguments, and you feel it's your job to stop them. Things get broken. Threats are made. People leave suddenly, and that can be a relief, but when they don't come back, you can't help but worry. If they come back, they usually don't want to go to bed, even if you do. You don't sleep well. During the best of times, you're preoccupied with the tension that comes from not knowing what's going to happen next.

Neither of my parents went to college and they were uncomfortable among people who did. I think they sensed that I considered an education my passport to independence, but they didn't want to appear to oppose me. So, for the record, they were proud that I went to college and privately they scorned me for it. I learned not to get caught reading *The New York Times* or using a word they didn't ordinarily use. If I expressed concern when they drank too much, they accused me of looking down on them and threatened to stop paying my tuition.

Facing Up to the Truth

On the day I graduated, I felt numb. The four years were over and I could finally make plans to get away. My parents were drunk when they came to the ceremonies, and I was especially embarrassed because their guests were a couple who didn't drink and didn't know what went on in our family. The couple had been very supportive of me and seemed genuinely proud that I was getting my degree. I wondered what they would think of me after they saw what I knew was going to happen when we all went out to dinner: the arguments, the abusive language, my parents' descent from a good-looking man and woman to disheveled drunks.

I had the wild notion that my parents deliberately chose their guests in order to cause me shame. But no, I told myself, they wouldn't do something as cruel as that.

Wouldn't they?

Never underestimate the cleverness of an alcoholic, even if he is your parent. If he is playing his game— and he plays it all the time—he will pick up on every word, every expression, every gesture, and use it to his advantage. You may not be aware of your needs and your feelings, but he is acutely sensitive to each one of them. You may wonder how a parent can be cruel to a child, but the alcoholic doesn't see things that way. He doesn't see his behavior as cruel, and he will be genuinely shocked if you tell him it is. He sees only his goal, which is to justify his drinking and be punished for it. As far as the game is concerned, you aren't his child; you're a means toward an end that he passionately desires.

If you find this shocking, if you cannot accept it, you are not alone. Our whole society is on your side. "One of the unwritten laws in our society is that you have to believe your parents are perfect," says Vincent Di Pascuale. "That comes to us through religion—it puts parents on a pedestal, and if you think there's something wrong with them, then there must be something wrong with *you*. We still don't understand that we can love someone and still be angry with that person.

"Then there's another unwritten law for families. It's called, 'Don't wash our dirty linen in public—because if you do, you're a traitor.'

"What you have to realize is that each person perceives life in his own way. That's why some children in a family will admit the parent is an alcoholic and some won't. But if you feel you were abused by your parents, then you did suffer abuse, no matter how anyone else looks at what happened to you. You're the one who perceived the abuse, and you're the one who now has to heal your perception through your recovery."

"ACOAs will minimize the most horrific things that happen to them," says Dr. Yvonne Kaye, herself the child of alcoholic parents and also a recovering alcoholic. "We don't want to tell anybody how rotten our parents are because—they're our *parents*, and we *want* them to be loving."

Claudia expressed those sentiments ferociously the first night she attended an ACOA self-help group. She listened impatiently as some of the others spoke of their limited success in maintaining a relationship with their alcoholic parents. Then she said, "I don't know how you can be satisfied with that."

"With what?" a blond young man asked.

"With not knowing that your parents love you," Claudia said.

"Sometimes parents don't," the young man said gently.

"That's not true in my case!" Claudia said, her voice rising. "My problem is getting my father to *admit* he loves me. I know he does, but he just doesn't act that way! My God, I've done everything I can to give him the opportunity. Do you want to know what I did? I'll tell you what I did! My father works for an airline and he travels a lot, and I thought maybe that was why he never came to see me. So I moved. I got an apartment only a few blocks from him and I told him, 'Now you don't have any more excuses not to see me.' He came around once. Only once in the past six months! He said he rang my bell and I wasn't home, I was working. But he knew I was working, so why did he come around when I wasn't there? Then I quit my job. And I told him, 'Now you can't say I wasn't home.' I'm home all the time, but he still never sees me." By then Claudia's hands were clenched and she was pummeling the table with the heels of her fists as she spoke.

Claudia is thirty-two and has been married five times. She is petite, stylishly dressed, and pretty, but her face is perpetually contorted into a frown. She's a computer programmer and doesn't have difficulty finding a job, which makes it easier for her to stop working when she wants to be more available to her father.

The group seemed to realize that she epitomized all their longings for the love of an alcoholic parent, and they were gentle with her. "What about the rest of your life, Claudia?" a tall, slim woman with short white hair asked. "Anything going on there?"

"There isn't any 'rest of my life,'" Claudia said. "I have to get this thing resolved with my father before I can do anything with my life." She said she had a boyfriend but wasn't ready to get married again. She wants to have children someday, but time is running out on her. She wants to stay long enough in a job to get somewhere. "But not until my father says he loves me!" she said. "He does! He does love me!"

It will be a long time before Claudia is able to realize that she has a life apart from her pursuit of a parent's love. And much longer before she is able to accept the fact that her father has no love to give. When the meeting ended, most of the group stopped to say a few words to her. They knew better than to put pressure on her, but they wanted to encourage her to attend more meetings. "Keep coming back—it really works," one woman promised.

"You have to go very slowly with an ACOA, because all their lives they've been pushed and prodded," advises Kathleen Diak, clinical coordinator of Breakthrough's Outpatient Program. "We try to give them the chance to tell us what *they* want to do. If they don't want to do something, that's okay with us. We want them to realize that they're okay as they are. If they want to make changes, then they should do it because there's something in it for them. It takes an ACOA a long time to get to that point of asking, 'What's in it for me?' They have to begin in small ways to assert themselves and claim their own needs."

Running Away Doesn't Help

I used to think it was my mother who held on to me, but I was the one who couldn't let go of her. Even after two marriages, I was still trying to win her love and make her happy. We couldn't get along. No matter how carefully I studied her and anticipated her moods, she always surprised me with angry outbursts and denunciation. Sometimes I stayed away from her for two or three years, but that was harder than seeing her because I thought of her constantly. I got an unlisted telephone number because she would call me in the middle of the night, drunk, and shout abuses at me. She called me at work instead, and if I wasn't at my desk she would tell the switchboard operator what a terrible daughter I was. More than once a police officer came to my door to tell me that my mother had called the station and asked for help in locating me because she was having a heart attack. It wasn't true, of course, but it brought me to the phone, and from there to a reconciliation. And each time the reconciliation lasted only long enough to suit my mother's needs. Running away didn't help me, and neither did running back. As long as I kept on hoping she would love me, I was bound to her.

Many ACOAs have similar experiences. The bonds are there even when an alcoholic parent ignores the child. And even when the parent dies. The only way to sever them is to love ourselves.

Getting Out of the Game

The turning point for me was not a sudden insight. It happened in stages, over a long period of time. It began several years ago when my mother was told she had bone cancer in her left leg. She was presented with alternative methods of treatment—chemotherapy or amputation of the leg—and she immediately chose amputation. I wasn't living near her at the time, but I was in touch with her and my stepfather by telephone several times a day. I was horrified when my mother refused to seek another opinion and did not want to wait for additional laboratory tests to confirm the diagnosis. She wanted the surgery performed as soon as possible, and it was done two days later. My stepfather went along with her decision, although he too thought she should have gotten a second opinion. "But," he said to me on the morning of the operation, "this way I'll still have her with me. Even is she can't walk, I can still talk to her."

My mother was not prepared in any way for the physical and psychological aftermath of an amputation. She had not considered how her everyday life would change when she could no longer stand without assistance or support. The recovery was long and very painful, but she endured it with a gallantry that brought tears of admiration to my eyes. By the time she left the hospital she was a favorite with the nurses and doctors and an inspiration to many other patients.

At home, she did everything her nurses and physical therapists told her to do. She exercised to strengthen the muscles in her arms so she could use a walker and crutches until it was time for her to learn how to use a prosthesis—and this was a woman who previously never walked two steps for her health. On her own she stopped drinking and cut down on her cigarettes. She taught my stepfather how to cook, and when she learned how to use a wheelchair she helped in the kitchen and insisted on doing the dishes after they ate. She was cheerful and optimistic.

One day, when I went to see her, she said she had a surprise for me. The prosthesis was in place and she wanted to show me how well she could walk from the living room to her bedroom. The distance was about fifteen paces and it took her twenty minutes to make it with the aid of her walker. As I watched her, agonizingly slow and sweat dripping off her forehead from the strenuous physical effort of coordinating her thigh muscles with the prosthesis, I knew I was seeing the real woman instead of the alcoholic. I never loved anyone so much in all my life. And the sight of her, at the age of seventy, smiling triumphantly when the journey was over, made me believe that something very good was coming out of all her suffering.

From that fifteen-pace beginning, my mother worked every day with a therapist to learn how to go up and down the stairs from her apartment to the first floor of the building. She learned how to get in and out of my stepfather's car. They even went out to lunch once. And then, without any debate or warning, she announced she would never wear the prosthesis again or leave her apartment. She said all that effort was stupid and a waste of time. When I called her the next morning, she was drunk. She continued to drink, and my stepfather fell back into his role of supplier because, he said, "What else does she have in life?"

I was not the only person who had unwittingly played the part of a rescuer. My mother's doctors, her nurses, and her therapists were shocked at her abrupt reversal into total physical helplessness. Her friends, who had been cheered by her courage, were stunned by her resignation. They all tried to change her mind. They all tried to reignite the sense of purpose and determination they had seen in her. They failed. She said nothing. She listened to them patiently, smiling that strange smile, and asked my stepfather to pour her a drink.

Dr. Claude Steiner, in his book *Games Alcoholics Play*, came very close to describing my mother's behavior in his analysis of a game he calls "Wino," the most destructive kind of alcoholic behavior: " 'Wino' is always part of a self-destructive life script. The thesis 'I'm no good, you're O.K. (ha, ha)' is translated here to 'I'm sick (try and avoid that), you're well (ha, ha).' The game of 'Wino' is played 'for keeps' because it uses body organs and tissue as counters.

" . . . In the game of 'Wino' . . . the Alcoholic obtains strokes by making himself physically ill. He is willing to sacrifice his bodily integrity to the point of putting his survival on the line, which practically forces others to take care of him . . . the Alcoholic is physically devastated and therefore entitled to some oral gratification—the payoff in this game. . . . To the alcoholic, the fact that he must be at death's door to get supplies from people implies that those other people, who are in positions of strength and power, are really not O.K."

I didn't try to change my mother's mind. I looked into her eyes and knew that, grotesque as it seemed, she was satisfied. I had seen that expression every time she played the game and won. I think that in her own mind she was being punished severely enough by the loss of her leg to last the rest of her life. If she had gone on with her recovery as gallantly as she began, there would have been no point in playing the game— and she couldn't give it up.

As for me, I had taken an important step in *not* trying, once again, to rescue her. And the only reason I didn't is that I was watching her through the eyes of my adult instead of through the eyes of a child desperate for love at any cost. I knew, for the first time in my relationship with my mother, that I didn't cause her suffering. But I actually felt the tug of guilt reaching out to the child, calling her to run to my mother's rescue. "No, don't go," my adult said to my child. "Stay here with me. This is something I have to handle." The guilt was gone. The child was protected. The adult understood what was happening. The game went on without me—and my mother knew it. From that day on, she began to look for other rescuers. They weren't hard to find.

My next important realization was that I couldn't make my mother happy, and that took a little longer. Three years after her surgery, on her seventy-third birthday, I thought of the perfect gift for her. I always put a lot of effort into selecting her gifts, but she usually exchanged them or put them away and didn't use them. This time I thought I could give her something she really might enjoy.

Before she confined herself to her apartment, my mother's greatest pleasure was dining out. So I called the owner of her favorite restaurant and arranged for two celebratory dinners to be delivered to my parents' home. I told my stepfather about my gift so that he wouldn't be taken by surprise when the doorbell rang. I was as excited as a child coming home from school with something I had made for my mother.

I talked to my mother on the morning of her birthday, but when I didn't hear from her the next day I began to think that something had gone wrong and the dinners weren't delivered. I was embarrassed to call and ask whether my gift arrived, but finally I had no choice.

"Oh, yes, we got the dinners," my mother said irritably, "and they were terrible."

"Why?" I asked. "What was wrong with them?"

"I just didn't like the whole idea, that's all," she said.

As hurt as I was by her rejection, I saw something I had missed before. By then I was benefitting from the steady support of the adult in me, and I knew I wasn't a wrong little kid. I was a pretty good little kid, and my gift was given in love. For once, my mother's rejection didn't change my perception of myself. I saw very clearly that I hadn't caused my mother's unhappiness and I couldn't make her happy. I didn't feel as if I had done something wrong and was being punished for it. I knew I had done something loving, but it wasn't accepted that way—which was okay. My mother had every right to feel however she wanted to feel about my gift, but that didn't change the fact that I was able to love her.

I wish I could say that when I began to see my mother more realistically, our relationship improved. But it didn't. It got much worse because my mother sensed immediately that I was beginning to let go of her. What did improve was my relationship with other people. Once I stopped expecting them to love me, it's amazing how much easier it was for me to be myself and let other people decide for themselves how they felt about me. This is what happens when we learn to love ourselves.

"We tell ACOAs ahead of time that when they begin to get better, when they begin to change their behavior, they're actually going to feel worse for a while," says Kathleen Diak. "That's because a lot of the people in their lives aren't going to like the changes. Certainly the alcoholics won't like them because the ACOA won't respond in the same old ways. Even among families, it often happens that brothers and sisters don't look at the alcoholic parent in the same way, and they'll be upset when the recovering ACOA begins to accept the reality of the situation. So we tell them, 'Anytime you try to get healthy, you're being disloyal to your family—and you're going to *feel* disloyal.' "

Guilt is always uncomfortable, Diak admits, "but if a person is in recovery, the guilt doesn't last. We advise people to ride out their anxieties during this transitional period. It's better for them just to be with these feelings and think about them for a while instead of reaching for a Valium. We explain to them that discomfort often is a sign of growth—it may mean that you're doing something out of your script—and that's good! If people know ahead of time what to expect when they begin to recover, that can help them deal with those sick feelings. And then, after a while, they really begin to feel much better."

A Few Rules to Remember

If you're trying to let go of a parent and you feel you're being lured back into the alcoholic's game, try to remember a few simple rules:

- When things go wrong, don't share them with your alcoholic parent. Remember that you're old enough to deal with them yourself or to get the help you need.
- When things go right, do the same thing. Share your happiness with someone who isn't threatened by it.
- When your alcoholic parents attack you, don't assume that you did something wrong and try to make it right. Do what's right for yourself and get out of their striking range.
- Take the pressure off the child in you to perform, to achieve, to be perfect in order to win your parent's approval. Just let the child be, and enjoy her company.
- When a problem arises, look at it realistically. Don't think, *How can I change this situation and make it right?* Think, *How am I going to deal with it as it is?*

It takes time to let go of an alcoholic parent, and it is never easy. Your vulnerability to guilt and accusations of wrongdoing will be tested, but if you fall back into old habits, don't be hard on yourself. The important thing is to catch yourself in the act and let your adult lead you into healthier behavior. If you find yourself hovering over your parent and ignoring your own needs, you know something is wrong. Pay attention to the signals; they come from the healthy child in you and she's telling you she needs you.

If you feel disloyal, don't do anything about it. Wait. Don't change what you're doing. In a few days you'll begin to feel better about yourself, and that may be something you've never experienced. It's the beginning of self-esteem and it will help you to look at yourself more objectively. Once that happens, you'll begin to realize that what you thought was disloyalty is actually something that is supposed to happen: You're growing up. Sometimes it hurts, but not for long.

CHAPTER SEVEN

EMBRACING THE TRUTH

NOT LONG AGO *alcoholism* was a bad word. Now it describes an illness that afflicts a large portion of our population. Education about its causes and treatment is beginning to change the way the public perceives alcoholics, and this in turn may eventually change the way ACOAs perceive themselves. Today the young child of an alcoholic may have a better chance to grow up with fewer emotional handicaps because the alcoholic himself has a better chance to be understood, accepted, and helped by our society. But if you are an adult child of an alcoholic, you grew up in a different, more prejudicial environment. You know what it is to suffer from association with a social outcast.

When you get to know them, alcoholics are unattractive people. They are emotionally volatile, often irrational and out of control, abusive, deceitful, neglectful, and self-absorbed. They aren't there when you need them, you can't depend on them for anything, and they can be dangerous. Although they like to portray themselves as harmless, jolly-good fellows, the truth is that they are destructive, depressing, and undesirable. They are the people most other people try to avoid.

The Need to Deny

Growing up as the child of an alcoholic is a torment-
ing experience. You're not blind to the truth, but you
aren't mature enough to handle it, and neither are the
others in your family, no matter what their age. You
sense very quickly that some people shy away from
your parent once they know the truth about him, and
you don't want that to happen to you. You're also torn
between revulsion at the alcoholic's behavior and your
normal desire to love your parent. When the truth
inflicts more pain than you can bear, you begin to tell
yourself that what you see really isn't there. And,
together with other members of your family, you cover
up for the alcoholic to reinforce your altered version of
the way things are. Because you're afraid that the
truth will destroy you, you try to survive by destroying it. Unfortunately, in the process, you do serious
damage to yourself.

Refusing to admit the truth about your alcoholic
parent, and consequently about the effects of alcoholism on your own development, is called *denial*. It's a
word you'll hear often in recovery. Like some other
words that are popular in treatment programs, it's a
simplified, rather clinical way of describing a complex, highly emotional experience that leaves scars.
Denial is the way an ACOA tries to deal with shame
and anger.

"We lived in a row house," says Martin, "and the
walls were thin. When my father came home drunk,
we'd all try to keep him quiet and hope the neighbors
wouldn't hear him, because then they'd know.

"I think my shame was one of the main reasons why
I became an accountant," he says. "I felt I'd get some
respect and dignity out of a suit and a tie."

Sara remembers the shame she felt when her father got drunk. "We lived in a small town and everybody knew everybody. My father was the postmaster, and people respected him. He was a fairly good artist, too, and I was very proud when they exhibited some of his paintings in the library one summer. But when he got drunk, I'd worry about what people would think if they found out. I loved my father, and it hurt to think that people might turn their backs on him. But I had a personal interest in what he did, too. The shame was especially painful when I was a teenager, because that's when you think the whole world is scrutinizing you."

The Power of a Word

Herb thinks his wife is crazy when she urges him to join a support group for ACOAs. He doesn't consider himself one of them. But don't refer to his father as an alcoholic if you want to stay on good terms with Herb. "Sure, he drank," he'll admit. "Sometimes he'd go off on a week-long bender, but that's not being an alcoholic. My father worked his ass off to support us, and there were seven of us. After my mother died, he kept us together as a family until we all grew up. No way was he an alcoholic!"

Herb is married, with two teenaged daughters. His wife thinks he ought to spend more time with them, especially now, when everybody worries about drugs. Herb says he loves his family, but he doesn't have much time for them. He works a lot of overtime at the printing plant where he's a supervisor. His wife wants to know why someone else, Herb's boss, for instance, can't carry some of the work load, but Herb says his boss depends on him to run the place. "I'm not trying to brag," Herb says, "but I'm the only one he can trust to do things right."

One reason why Herb works so hard is that he's a perfectionist. He'll stay with a print order all night if he isn't satisfied, but when it's done he feels kind of empty inside. "Just once I wish I could look at a job and be proud I did it. But I'm not. I'm always afraid somebody will find something wrong that I missed."

At home Herb is always tearing down a wall or putting one up. He considers himself a responsible husband, and his wife agrees, but she wishes they could go away for a few days, just the two of them. "We never talk," she says. "We're like two polite strangers."

"Would you rather fight?" Herb teases.

"Maybe," his wife says. "Maybe then we'd get things out in the open."

Herb shakes his head and picks up his toolbox. "There's nothing to get out," he says, turning toward the stairs. "We're fine the way we are."

His wife isn't sure. Herb's oldest brother died a few months ago in a plane crash, and Herb hasn't allowed himself to grieve. "I don't expect him to go to pieces," his wife says, "but he needs to talk about it. They were very close, like best friends, and I know Herb misses him. He acts as if it didn't happen, but he can't possibly feel that way."

If you were to suggest to Herb that his emptiness, his perfectionism, his rigidity in the face of grief, his inability to enjoy life, and his reluctance to trust people with his feelings are characteristics of an adult child of an alcoholic, he would say you're crazy. But until he can admit that you may have a point, his life won't get any better.

"Many ACOAs don't know they have problems because they don't want to admit that their parents had problems," says Kathleen Diak. "They just feel that their lives are meaningless. Many have a hard time perceiving a parent as an alcoholic, but until that happens, no recovery is possible."

"On Sunday afternoons, when my father took us to the VFW, I'd sit there with my soda and wonder why those same few men were there every week," Sara remembers. "Where were the rest of the VFW's? Were they home with their families? Then it dawned on me that my father and his drinking friends were all hiding out there from their families. Their wives couldn't get to them because the VFW didn't allow women in those days. The only reason I was allowed, I guess, was that I was just a kid, so that didn't count.

"I'd sit there and think, *My God, my father's an alcoholic!* Then I'd feel guilty for even thinking the word because nobody else in my family would say it.

"When you can't use words honestly, when you have to keep them secret, they have power over you. A word like *alcoholic*, if you can't say it openly, makes you feel guilty and ashamed just for thinking it, as if you did something bad. It also makes you judgmental toward other people. I remember how I felt when the men would start to sing. They were so loud, such hypocrites—their favorite song, and they'd sing it four or five times, was 'Mother Macree,' and when they came to the line, 'God bless you and keep you, Mother Macree,' I'd think, *You bastards! You probably put her in her grave!*

"It wasn't the word *alcoholic* that tyrannized me. It was the fact that I couldn't say it to anyone. If an alcoholic was so terrible that I had to keep it a secret, then what would people think about *me* if they found out about my father?

"Once I stopped hiding the truth, once I started saying, 'My father is an alcoholic,' the word stopped scaring me. It didn't have any more power over me, because I knew it was just a word. There was more to my father than his alcoholism, but the alcoholism was there. It was part of his life. But I had to find out what it meant in *my* life."

Looking the Other Way

The children of alcoholics didn't invent denial. Neither did their families. They took their cues from the rest of society.

I remember so many people who looked the other way when my parents drank. Their relatives, the people who worked with them, the friends who weren't drinking buddies—how many times they saw my parents struggle through a morning after, or sat in the same room with them, watching them become incoherent and even violent, yet behaving as if they were perfectly normal. Even more oblivious were the doctors who treated the aftermath of their drunkenness and called it by other names. Years later some of those people could say to me, "Sure, we knew they were alcoholics. Didn't you know we knew?" I didn't. And it would have helped if I had. I would have known I wasn't "imagining" things. I might have been less afraid of the truth if I didn't have to face it alone.

But perhaps I'm being unfair. I'm forgetting how difficult it is to confront an alcoholic.

"You certainly don't want to confront an alcoholic when he's drinking," explains Dr. Paul J. Fink, chairman of the Department of Psychiatry of Albert Einstein Medical Center and president of the American Psychiatric Association. "You never know what he'll do. And if you confront him when he's not drinking, you may drive him to drink."

Dr. Fink agrees that "There has been a tremendous

tendency to deny alcoholism. In a society that sanctions drinking, it's very easy to make believe the drinking is not pathological. We make excuses. We say the person drinks a little . . . it's not such a terrible thing . . . he's tired at the end of the day, so he has five martinis . . . it's not such a big deal—everybody drinks a little . . . he's a social drinker."

In the business world, where alcoholism eats away at productivity and profits, denial is also at work. "Sure, the alcoholic may show up on time, but very often he's just not with it," Dr. Fink says. "He makes excuses—he didn't sleep well, he had a fight with his wife, his car broke down—and we buy into them. We don't want to mind other people's business. That's part of our culture, too: We're not supposed to intrude on other people's space. It's also easier that way. Telling somebody, 'You know, Joe—or Mary—I think you're an alcoholic,' is like telling somebody he has bad breath. You might get a punch in the nose."

Only once did Elizabeth confront her father about his drinking. "I was about sixteen," she says. "We were sitting down to Sunday dinner and he spilled his drink. He thought it was funny and he bent over and began to lick the wine up with his tongue. He was so drunk! I looked at my mother and saw that she was shaking, but she didn't say a word. That's when I stood up and said to my father, 'I hate you! Why do you have to drink all the time? Why can't you be like other people?'

"He sat up and glared at me. I thought he was going to kill me, but I was so scared I couldn't move. Then he bunched up the ends of the tablecloth in his fists and pulled the whole thing—plates, food and all—onto himself, the floor, and everything else. He stood up and began to stomp on the plates that hadn't broken. It was a nightmare!"

"Anyone who tries to stop the alcoholic from being

bad will end up feeling definitely not O.K., feeling either foolish or angry," advises Dr. Claude Steiner.

A Shift Toward Acceptance

The social environment that made denial possible and, at times, necessary to survival, began to change slowly. In 1935 two alcoholics who proved they could sober up founded Alcoholics Anonymous, a self-help organization that challenged the prevailing belief that an alcoholic was a loathesome bum who didn't have the willpower to stop drinking. AA is still the most influential and best-known source of recovery for alcoholics.

In 1957 the American Medical Association declared alcoholism a disease, a statement that implied three major changes in the way alcoholics are perceived:

- Alcoholics are not to blame for their condition.
- Their condition can and should be treated.
- The cost of treatment, like the cost of treatment for other declared diseases, should be covered by medical insurance programs.

The long-range effect of this declaration has been:

- The realization that an alcoholic is not an immoral scourge, but a human being who needs and deserves help
- The growth of a large and profitable addiction rehabilitation industry

Alcoholics Anonymous led the way in making the public aware that the families of alcoholics were also afflicted by the disease. It began offering self-help programs to family members and friends through its affiliates, Al-Anon and Al-a-Teen. In 1974 the term "Adult Children of Alcoholics" came into use as researchers found that the effects of an alcoholic parent stayed with the child into adulthood.

"In the last ten years we've seen a shift toward the acceptance and treatment of alcoholism," says Dr. Paul Fink. "Today people talk openly and freely about going to their AA and Al-Anon meetings, and about being in therapy. The treatment of alcoholism and drug addiction can be very costly, but more states are mandating insurance coverage for it.

"In the business world, there is a serious effort to understand that employees who are alcoholics can still make valuable contributions to the corporation. About twenty years ago Employee Assistance Programs— EAPs—were started, first for alcoholism, then for drug addiction, alcoholism and mental illness. These are confidential case-findings within corporations. A supervisor sees somebody who appears to be on drugs or alcohol and takes him aside and says, 'Hey, Joe—or Mary—maybe you ought to go to EAP.' Now, that's a lot easier and much more effective than saying, 'You're an alcoholic,' or 'You're an addict.' Then the employee calls a private number and arranges to see a counselor elsewhere. The counselors try to steer people into treatment and rehab programs.

"A change I consider very important is the strong public-education activity that links alcoholism with some of its bad results. Warnings like 'Don't drink and drive' help people to understand that alcoholism is not an innocent issue, but one with implications and fallout."

Breakthrough's Kathleen Diak cautions that the changes in the way people perceive alcoholics have not yet reached many areas of our society. She also points out that "labeling alcoholism a disease isn't acceptable to some people, and very often they are the people most in need of help. If the child of an alcoholic is into denying that there's anything wrong with his parent, then calling alcoholism a disease isn't going to get through to him. He still won't want to admit that his parents have a disease because they still don't want anybody to know about it. If he does admit it, he feels disloyal. Loyalty is an important part of denial. It's one of the reasons why the alcoholic's family doesn't seek outside help. They think it's their responsibility to take care of the alcoholic, and by the time they realize that they can't, they're too exhausted to try a new approach."

Diak thinks that our changing attitudes toward alcoholism may eventually make it easier for ACOAs to accept the truth about their parents without feeling disloyal. "If they can see that admitting the truth is a step toward getting help for an alcoholic parent, they'll feel better about taking that step. But ACOAs will have to get past some of their own denial before they can benefit from some of these social changes."

Vincent Di Pascuale of The Starting Point does not think society is ready to stop denying that alcoholism and other forms of addiction are destroying people's lives. "It's a matter of economics," he says. "In our country, drugs and alcohol are big business, and we're not about to give that up. Our economy is based on addiction—we thrive on people being sick and we, knowingly or unknowingly, try to make them sicker. We try to create appetites in people for the things we want to sell—we do it to children.

"We live in a consumer-oriented world that glamorizes all kinds of addictions: smoking, drinking, eating, drugs, money, clothing, gadgets, all kinds of material things. We're not a playing society, but when we play, our fun and games are based on addictions—look at all the beer commercials that interrupt your ballgames on TV! We don't emphasize holistic health—how to eat well, think well, get in touch with your feelings, and know who you are. Instead we push an addictive kind of health. You can't just exercise, you have to wear the right kind of clothes, use the right equipment, go to the right fitness club. You can't just be healthy, you have to make yourself beautiful and enticing. You can't just eat a well-balanced meal, you have to think about food all the time. You can't go two blocks without coming to a fast-food restaurant that makes it easy for you to stuff yourself.

"Sure, there are changes in the way some people look at the alcoholic, but they're small changes. Looking at alcoholism and drug addiction honestly, and then trying to do something about them on a big scale, means we'd have to change our whole economic foundation. And that's another ballgame entirely. We look the other way because we don't want to give up our own addictions to power and money."

How We Can Stop Denying

Telling ACOAs that society is learning to accept the alcoholic isn't going to help; we can't wait that long. We also can't change the fact that our parents are alcoholics. So what can we do? How can we find the courage to live with the truth?

Try a little stop-action on yourself the next time you feel ashamed of your alcoholic parent. *Why* are you ashamed? You know you can't change the fact that your parent is drunk, so you know better than to wish she weren't. But are you hoping no one you know sees her that way? Are you more concerned about your own image than your parent's?

What people think is very important to ACOAs. We

work hard to make a good impression, to win approval, but an alcoholic parent can wipe it out in seconds. And that leaves us feeling like wrong little kids again, doesn't it? That's what shame does to us. It makes us feel wrong. It hurts.

If you've come this far with me, you know you can't feel any worse, so why not try something radical? What can you lose?

Try calling out for the adult in you, because that's what you ought to do anytime you feel this way. When you're down as far as you can go, it means you panicked. It means the child in you didn't wait for the adult to take charge and ran headlong into a situation she can't handle. You're out of your league, baby, but I say that with affection.

Let your adult deal with your shame. By now you must realize that your adult doesn't care who your parent is or what she does. He cares about you. A wonderful storybook parent isn't going to make him love you more, and an alcoholic parent isn't going to turn him away. Your adult deals in truth, and he knows who you are. He doesn't expect you to be perfect, and he knows you're not terrible. He's not interested in labels. You're just you, and that's fine with him.

There is nothing shameful about truth. It simply is. It's neutral. It won't hurt you, either. Denying is what hurts, because it's looking at truth through the eyes of the alcoholic and catching the alcoholic's fear of it. Look at truth through your eyes—your adult's eyes— and you'll see what it really is: freedom from your bondage to shame. If you let your adult love you and appreciate you, you'll know you're okay. And when you're okay, you won't care what anybody else does or thinks or expects. When you're okay, you don't need anyone's approval because you have your own. And when you don't need approval, you can't be damaged by someone else's behavior. That's why shame can't touch you if you're being yourself.

People will still think whatever they want to think. You can't stop them. Some will turn away from you because they want to avoid your alcoholic parent and they'll assume you're just like him. But you'll know you're you, so what do you care? You haven't lost a friend, because a friend would be able to tell the difference between your parent and you. You've only lost somebody who can't admit the truth, another deny-er. Look for a friend somewhere else. Look for someone who sees you through his own eyes. You don't need anyone to define you—you can do that for yourself.

ACOAs deny the truth about our parents because we want to deny the truth about ourselves: We're ashamed of our parents and we're angry at them. These are uncomfortable feelings, but if we can acknowledge them, understand them, and put them to rest, we won't have any reason to fear the truth. Learning to appreciate our uniqueness—defining ourselves—is half of the battle against denial. Letting go of our anger is the other half. But that's a chapter in itself.

CHAPTER EIGHT

LISTEN TO YOUR ANGER

SOME ACOAS CAN'T TALK about their childhood because they don't remember it. Some can't remember parts of it. Doug says that every now and then an incident comes back to him, but most of his early years are a blank. In many of these lives, forgetting is like a mercy killing meant to end the pain. But it doesn't end the anger. That's something we try to do by denying it. The result is that we're angry, we don't know why, and we tell ourselves we're not angry at all. That's enough to make anyone sick, and many of us do get physically and emotionally sick because we're angry and can't admit it.

"Denial causes a lot of psychosomatic complaints in adult children of alcoholics," says Kathleen Diak. "They often have gastrointestinal problems, headaches, depression, fatigue—their anger has nowhere else to go."

For many years I was plagued with asthma attacks that usually accompanied a bad cold, but sometimes they seemed to come out of nowhere. I would feel a severe tightness in my chest, as if I had taken a deep breath and couldn't exhale it. A doctor explained to me that that was exactly what asthma is: being able to breathe in, but not out. The air gets trapped in the lungs and bronchial passages and exerts tremendous pressure, but in the meantime you're still taking in more air, because by now you're panicky and breathing faster. You feel like a balloon about to burst, and eventually you can't breathe in, either.

[145]

In time the threat of these attacks began to rule my life. I was afraid to go anywhere out of reach of my doctor, because when I needed help, I needed it right away. As the attacks became more frequent, they exhausted me physically and I always felt tired. Exercise was something I avoided.

One day, when my doctor had almost run out of ideas for treatment, he gave me something to consider. He told me that asthma is sometimes induced or made worse by the suppression of rage, and he asked me if I was angry about something. "Not just angry," he said, "but *furious*."

I shook my head wearily. I wasn't angry about anything, I said. Everything was fine. What a lie!

My doctor thought it would be a good idea for me to see a psychiatrist anyway, just to explore the possibility that part of my problem wasn't physical. It couldn't hurt, he said. That was the beginning of a long, on-and-off association with a few excellent therapists who helped me to see that much of my life needed to be explored, understood, and healed. It took a few years for me to get around to the rage, but it certainly was there, and as I began to deal with it, my health improved dramatically.

I had trouble remembering my first asthma attack, but when I finally did, I could understand why I had tried to wipe it out of my memory. I was twenty years old, and it was the Christmas season. I had had a bad cold for over a week and I was cramming for my midterms, so I wasn't getting much sleep. My mother wanted me to meet her after work one evening to go Christmas shopping and then meet my stepfather at a restaurant for a late dinner. It was something we did every year, and I didn't have the courage to get out of it. I knew my mother didn't like to go anywhere by herself, and I didn't want her to know how awful I felt because she accused me of looking for sympathy whenever I was sick. So I went shopping with her, and it wasn't long before I knew I was in trouble. For the first time in my life, I couldn't seem to breathe properly. I actually had to concentrate on taking air in and pushing it out. It scared me, and being scared made it harder for me to breathe.

We shopped until the stores closed and then we met my stepfather. My mother had been looking forward to her first martini all evening, and she drank several of them with her dinner. My stepfather had a few beers.

When we came home, I went to my room and lay down on my bed, but when I heard my mother coming down the hall, I sat up. She had come to tell me something, but when she looked at me, she asked me why I was so pale. "You're white as a sheet," she said, and before I could answer, she said, "I knew you'd do something like this. You didn't fool me. I knew you didn't want to come with me tonight. All you care about is yourself. You don't care about me at all. And now you're trying to make me think you're dying just to make me feel bad!"

I opened my mouth to tell her that wasn't true, but the words never came out. I couldn't get air out or in, and a strange, rasping sound struggled out of my throat. I was terrified and I stood up, trying to force some of the trapped air out of my lungs. I wanted to scream for help, but my voice wasn't there. I felt as if I were drowning, and each second seemed to last forever. Finally, as my room was beginning to recede from me, I forced the air out, and with it came a rush of tears.

My mother was frightened. She had called for my stepfather and he stood in the doorway with her. The two of them seemed afraid to come near me. As I sat down on the bed, sobbing with relief, I still couldn't talk. My chest felt tight, and I breathed carefully and slowly, hoping I wouldn't stop breathing again. Then my mother put her hand on my head and told me I didn't have a fever.

"Should I call a doctor?" my stepfather said.

"Yes," my mother told him. "I think she's having a heart attack."

Within a few minutes we were on our way to a doctor. My mother and I sat in the back of the car and she put her arms around me. She tried to pull my head down on her shoulder, as if I were a little girl, but it was hard for me to breathe unless I sat up straight, and she was offended when I pulled away from her. "No one will ever love you as much as I do," she said. She often said that.

At the doctor's office I was told that my heart was sound but I had a respiratory problem. A shot of Adrenalin eased the pressure in my chest, and after I began breathing normally again I felt like celebrating.

On the way home my mother said nothing. As I tried to kiss her good night, she turned her face away and said, "Well, you really put us through hell tonight. I hope you're satisfied."

I didn't know what to say, and I didn't want to cry.

"I thought sure you had a heart attack," she went on. "God, all you had was a cold! Do you know what I do when I have a cold? I go to work, I come home and cook, I do the laundry, and make a nice home for everybody—but I don't act up and run to a doctor!"

I went to my room and closed the door, but I could hear her saying the same things to my stepfather in the living room. Then I heard her open the cabinet door where the liquor was kept. I was hurt and angry because my parents weren't there for me when I needed them. I was hurt and angry because they saw me as a deceiver, as a conniving, selfish child who would do anything to get her parents' attention. I wished I *had* had a heart attack. I wished it had killed me. And sometime after that, I wiped the wishes and the entire event out of my memory because I didn't know what to do with such feelings. In our family they weren't allowed.

I don't have asthma attacks anymore. But occasionally my breathing becomes a little labored, and that tells me something. Usually it means I have been ignoring what my child is trying to tell me: I'm angry. Something is wrong in my life, and I'd better do something about it. And when I do, I feel fine.

Pay Attention to Your Anger

It's hard for a child of an alcoholic to get angry. That's one of your handicaps. You may seem to be even-tempered, unemotional, but there's plenty of anger inside you and you don't dare let it out. That was one of the taboos in your childhood: You were never allowed to be angry at your parents, no matter what they did, even if they abused and neglected you. Being angry would have meant you thought they did something wrong, and they refused to be wrong. The slightest display of your anger could provoke dire reactions: verbal abuse, physical abuse, cruel deprivations, disappointments, unbearable guilt. Eventually you protected yourself by forgetting what made you angry, or by denying it ever happened. By the time you grew up, you couldn't get angry at anyone.

But the anger stayed in you and sometimes it made you sick. Maybe you were depressed. Maybe you were ill. Or maybe you broke some laws or totaled a car. Maybe you drank or took drugs to quiet the anger. But the worst part is that you couldn't admit to yourself that you were angry—especially at your parents.

Anger doesn't go away by itself. You have to do something to get rid of it. But what?

Acknowledge it. Bring your anger into the open. Anger is a very important message from the child in you. He's saying, "I'm hurt—help me!"

Pay attention to the pain. If your child got hurt, then he deserves your attention and care. Never mind what you were brought up to believe. In order to recover, you have to deal with reality, and the reality of this situation is that you got hurt. Don't let anyone tell you to forget it, ignore it, or that it didn't hurt. Your adult knows better; let your child know, too. Pay attention to the child's wounds. Comfort him, bind the wounds, sit with the child until he recovers. That's how the pain ends.

Give yourself permission to be angry. Love the child enough to accept *all* his emotions, the ugly as well as the beautiful. Most of the emotions he wasn't allowed to express were ugly, but they are the ones that must be faced first. They are valid emotions, valid responses to some ugly things that happened, and in the past they couldn't be expressed safely. But now you have a responsible, caring adult to look after the child and protect him from harm. He has a right to his ugly feelings, but he has been told for so long that he doesn't. Let him claim them now, and he'll be able to claim life's more pleasant emotions. At the right time, because he is basically a loving human being, he will be able to forgive the hurt that was inflicted on him. But first he must be given the freedom to admit how badly he was hurt—and be healed.

Keep listening to the child. If he trusts you enough to tell you how he feels, you must always honor those feelings. Whether it's a big hurt or a little hurt, stop what you're doing and listen. Don't tell him you'll take care of everything as soon as you can and then leave the child to take care of himself. That's the way his life used to be; don't let it be that way anymore. Give him comfort when he needs it, hold him close when he's scared. You can learn something from him: how to become the nurturing parent you never had and will always need.

How Angry Can You Get?

Loving your child means letting him know that it's okay for him to get angry—at anyone, and even in front of anyone. But once you do that, you have to make an important decision: What are you going to do with your anger? How are you going to express it? Are you going to attack the next person who makes you angry? Are you going to say what's on your mind? Are you going to have a good, cleansing cry? Get drunk? Go out and have a good time? Get even? You have a lot of options.

If you love yourself, you'll be all right. You'll be able to evaluate your options and consider the consequences of any action you choose to take. You'll look out for your own well-being. It's only when you don't love yourself that you're likely to do something foolish, harmful, or self-destructive.

Maybe you're wondering, Why bother about something that happened so long ago? The answer is that, inside you, where your anger is imprisoned, the cause of it never is old. It might as well have happened two minutes ago, because that's how much it still hurts. And, given the slightest opening, your anger will come out when you least expect it and often in inappropriate ways.

Sara can't remember being angry in her childhood, "but I made up for it later. Not long after I was married, the women's movement started, and it awakened me to so many things that were wrong in my life. I saw that I was stuck at home, with no money of my own and no power in my marriage. I had an education I worked very hard to get, and I wasn't able to use it. I was supposed to treat my husband as if he were a little boy and I was his new mother. I *hated* it! We were living with my in-laws then, and I saw my mother-in-law doing the same thing. So did my mother. And I blamed everything on men, my husband in particular. My reaction was way out of proportion, because my husband's a nice guy, and for a couple of years he put up with my anger and neither one of us knew where it came from. But all he had to do was walk in the door and I'd be furious. It wasn't the women's movement—that made me aware of my anger, but didn't cause it. I was angry because my father killed himself by drinking. I was angry at all the things that go with living in an alcoholic's home—at my mother for covering up for him, at my brother and sister for denying the way he was, at myself for the shame I felt.

"Then one day I said to myself, 'Do I *have* to keep doing things this way? Do I have to *go on* being a victim?' When I realized that I could change, I began to do things that were important to me. I began to teach, because that was something I wanted to do before I got married. I started asking my husband—and my children, too, when they were big enough—to help me run the house. Independence and self-sufficiency were important to me, so when we bought a little piece of land and built a summer house on it, I learned to do all the things my husband did, including climbing up on the roof and nailing the shingles—and I'm afraid of heights!

"It was getting past my anger that really freed me to be myself."

Kathleen Diak says that expressing anger is like going through a grieving process. "ACOAs didn't have a childhood, they didn't have love, and those are serious losses. There's a lot of pain associated with them.

Acknowledging it is like going through a period of mourning, and that's painful, too.

"One way to express your anger is to write down what you hate about your alcoholic parent. On a piece of paper, start with 'What I hate most about you is . . . ,' and go on from there. Getting your anger down on paper is very helpful because you're actually *doing* something with it, yet you're not hurting yourself or anyone else."

Mary Hoffman of Caron Counseling Services says, "It's a good idea to express your anger in a safe, protected place." Caron provides an "anger room" furnished with big, soft pillows and lightweight bats, which ACOAs can use to discharge their pent-up rage. "The room is almost soundproof, so you can yell as loud as you want."

"When I get really angry," Dr. Yvonne Kaye says, "I send my son out of the house, close the windows, draw the shades, and grab a big Turkish towel and start twisting it. Then I just yell. Sometimes I'll go out in my car and sit there with the windows closed and scream."

Fran still has some difficulty confronting people, especially her husband. "When I first realized how much anger I had in me, I was like a loaded gun, and my husband was usually the one who just happened to pull the trigger. So now, when I feel myself getting angry with him about something, I go off by myself and have an imaginary confrontation with him. That helps me to see whether the cause of my anger is something important and in the present, or something dredged up out of the past by some silly little thing that just happened. If it's important and in the present, I'll go and talk to my husband about how I feel. If it's something from the past, then I'm the one who has to deal with it."

"At Breakthrough we encourage ACOAs to express

anger as it arises in their present life—but to do it appropriately," Kathleen Diak explains. "For instance, if you're angry at your boss, you can't just walk in and tell him off. But you can find a private place where you can shout your feelings without losing your job. If you can express your anger before it builds up a lot of pressure inside you, then you can begin to do something about the situation that's causing the anger."

Is it Okay to Hate a Parent?

"Once an ACOA's anger about an alcoholic parent begins to come out, it can be pretty terrible," says Dr. Kaye."Many of them begin to hate their parents so much that they don't want to give it up. In some of their meetings, they'll talk about the way their parents treated them when they were children, and someone may say, 'Yes, but your parent was sick. Alcoholism is a disease, and your parent couldn't help the way he was because he was sick.' I've seen some ACOAs walk right out of the room if you say that. They don't want to hear about a disease. They just want to hold on to their hate because it's taken such a long time for them to admit it."

Sara warns that the label ACOA can make you feel "like Marley's ghost in *A Christmas Carol*—you know, dragging your chains around with you for the rest of your life. Sure, you have to get your anger out, and it's good to punch pillows and scream your head off, but you can get stuck there, too. You can make a career of being an ACOA, and some of us do. But you can't hit pillows and yell all the time. You can't live in a state of crisis all the time—the human body just won't tolerate that. So what else are you going to do with your life now that you know you're angry?

"After I spent a couple of years being angry, it suddenly dawned on me that I was addicted to it. I was like an alcoholic, and before I could make some changes in my life, I had to get the poison out of my system in the same way the alcoholic has to sober up. I had to give up the anger."

Yvonne Kaye says, "I tell my patients that it's all right to hate your parent for a reasonable length of time, but then you have to go on from there. It's important to distinguish *what* we hate. We don't hate the parent—we hate the disease. Our parents couldn't help being sick, so we can't hate them for that. But they could have got help for themselves, and if they didn't, *that's* what we hate."

"For a long time I thought I hated my father," Sara recalls, "but now I know that I didn't. I can look back and see so many things that I loved about my father— his warmth and affection for my mother and us, his sense of humor, his love of art, his gentleness. I hated the alcohol."

Kathleen Diak says, "It helps you to forgive if you can look at your parent honestly and see what was good in him. Don't try to alter what he was, because that won't work. But very often you'll find that you missed some good qualities because they were overshadowed by so many negatives."

At one point in my recovery I found it helpful to look back in that way. I had grown up trying to idolize my mother because that was what she expected of me. But after I began to admit my anger at her, I felt I had gone too far in the opposite direction. My mother was neither a saint nor a monster. She was a very sick, very disturbed woman who did a great deal of damage, not only to me but to many other people, but she was a human being. I thought I had better try to see her at least somewhat objectively because I am her daughter and she lives on in me, and I don't want to hate part of myself because it resembles her. So I began to seek out some of my more elusive memories of her. It helped.

My mother was a very determined woman. When I was in grammar school and needed a colonial woman's costume for a school program, she didn't buy one at the dime store. She didn't like what she saw there; she said they were cheesy, which was her most derogatory expression. She made me a costume—by hand, because she didn't have a sewing machine—and it was authentic right down to the curls in the wig because she went to the library to research it. When it was finished, she said no one appreciated how hard she worked and she got very drunk—but that doesn't cancel out her determination and effort. She was tough-minded and hardworking. As a very young girl she dropped out of high school and took a secretarial course so she could get a job and move out of a home that was unbearable. Between her first and second marriages, she supported herself, a full-time housekeeper, and me. She was witty, lively, and she loved to dance. She was always bringing home stray dogs and then never knew what to do with them. What I like most about her is that she liked to read. I can honestly say that I loved weekday nights during the years when my parents drank only on weekends, because both my mother and my stepfather always read after dinner. Without either of them saying a word, it was the warmest form of communication they ever seemed to achieve.

In many ways I am quite different from my mother, and at last I know it isn't wrong to be myself. But in some ways I am like my mother, and that used to bother me. In fact, I hated those characteristics. Now I'm beginning to appreciate them, because I realize I can choose how to express them. Enjoying the company of friends doesn't mean I have to get drunk. Working hard isn't a form of punishment; it can be an exciting challenge. Achieving a goal can be a pleasure in itself; nobody has to cheer. Looking after people makes me feel good about myself; it doesn't have to make me a martyr. I wish I could adopt all the animals in the world, but I can take good care of only one dog and one cat.

In some respects, finding the positives in my mother made her alcoholism even more tragic. I couldn't help but imagine what kind of a woman she might have become. . . . But they also gave me something to hold on to, something to love in my own way. They proved to me that I was not foolish to try to love her when I was a child; my mistake was expecting her to love me back.

Linda Gray Sexton speaks for many ACOAs who remember their alcoholic parents with conflicting emotions. "I wanted to be a wonderful mother because I didn't have a wonderful mother. I wanted to make it all over, to rewrite it, not just for the kids but for myself. To show that I could do this; I could do what [my mother] couldn't do. And what did I find out? I found out how many ways I *was* like her, which was crushing and overwhelming. I don't love every single minute of being with two little kids, so I'm not with them all day. It's hard, it's boring. Now I've come to accept that I can be like [my mother] in some ways without having to be like her in all ways."

Referring to her own career as a writer, Sexton says it has helped her to realize why writing was such an important part of her mother's life. But while she accepts the commitment her work exacts from her, she rejects the craziness her mother associated with it. About her most recent novel, which she describes as autobiographical, she says, "I couldn't have done it without her. And I couldn't have done it with her."

When It's Time to Forgive

Martin tries not to see his alcoholic father, but sometimes he can't avoid him. "He has dinner with us on Thanksgiving and Christmas. That's the only time my children see my father, because I don't want them to have to put up with him.

"Every year the same thing happens. I have a good relationship with my mother, and I see her all the time, and she never asks why I don't see my father. Except on Christmas. She'll always take me aside and say, 'Marty, he's your father. Can't you be a little nice to him?' And I always tell her, 'No, Ma, I can't. He was a lousy father, and I can't forget that! He's still a lousy father, even without the booze.' And it's true! My mother's had a rotten life with him and I don't know why she stays. I've told her that if she ever wants to leave him, she's got a home with us."

Marian says she and her alcoholic mother are reconciled. "She's been so alone since my father died, and I can't help feeling sorry for her. My father did everything for her, and she's the kind of woman who needs someone with her. She isn't drinking right now, but she's stopped before and it didn't last. I try to see her often, and I do little things for her when I can, so she'll know I'm there for her.

"I don't want to look back. I don't like to remember some of the things she did to my sister and me when we were little. She couldn't even look at us without hitting us, and not just slaps, either. Once she started hitting us, she couldn't stop, and then she'd cry so hard when she saw what she'd done to us. But we weren't supposed to cry. We were supposed to stand there and take it. That went on until I was in high school, and one night she came at me for no reason at all and I knew I wasn't going to let her hurt me. I was taller than she was by then and I guess I was stronger, too, because I caught both her arms and pushed her away as hard as I could. She lost her balance and fell down, and that was the last time she ever tried to hit me or my sister.

"Memories like that still hurt, but I have to remember that my mother was sick and didn't know what she was doing. She did the best she could—anyway, that's all in the past.

"She still knows how to upset me, though. I'm a lawyer, and I have a family, so I don't have much time. But I do a lot of things for my mother. I see her almost every day, even if it's only for a few minutes, and I often take her shopping on Saturdays. But she says I neglect her, and that makes me feel terrible. I keep telling myself I shouldn't expect her to say thanks or to let me know she loves me, because she never could do those things."

If you can't forgive your alcoholic parent, you're in trouble. But telling yourself that you've forgiven your parent, when you really haven't, is trouble, too. Withholding forgiveness may be your way of punishing your parent for not loving you. Or saying you forgive without going through the process of forgiveness may mean you're still hoping your parent will love you. Either way, you're still playing the alcoholic's game, even if you tell yourself you aren't, because what you do and what you are still depend upon what the alcoholic does. It won't do you any good to turn your back on your parent if he can still get into your head. And if you insist that you're getting along with your parent, but you're letting him hurt you, you're kidding yourself. You don't forgive by turning your back or knuckling under. Forgiveness is something that takes place in you alone. Your parent has nothing to do with it.

"Forgiveness is essential to recovery," Kathleen Diak says, "but it's different for different people. Sometimes a parent is dead. Sometimes a parent is an active alcoholic and can't be approached. We don't always advise a reconciliation because we don't think it's always realistic."

Maybe you're trying too hard to forgive. Maybe you're in too much of a hurry. Maybe some of your old guilt is putting pressure on you to let bygones be bygones and give your parent a big hug. Maybe you're falling back into your old pattern of trying to win your parent's approval. Maybe you feel like a wrong little kid again. Some of your friends in recovery groups may be urging you to reconcile with your parent because they want to do it, too, and they'd like some company to make them feel they're doing the right thing. If any or all of the above are pushing you to say you forgive your alcoholic parent, don't do it. You're not ready to forgive. You still hurt too much.

How can you heal the pain? Not all at once, to be sure. But it will begin to go away from the moment you take a step toward loving yourself. You'll always have the memory of the pain when you choose to recall it, because it's part of the truth, and you know how to live with the truth now. But the pain itself will go away as your adult begins to give the child in you the genuine love he never had.

As you learn to depend on yourself for the love you need, you will naturally begin to give up your agonizing dependency on your alcoholic parent—because it isn't good for you, and you will want what's good for you. As you become aware that you can love, that you deserve love, but that your parents can't love you, you will stop offering them opportunities to hurt you. And then you can begin to explore forgiving them, not because it's your duty or because you want their approval, but because forgiveness is what *you* need to break free of the past. It's your way of saying, "It's over."

Don't push it. Take your time. And realize that while your forgiveness may mean nothing to your parents, it will mean a lot to you and your future relationships. Your parents may not even know you've forgiven them—they may not believe there is anything to forgive—so don't imagine a tearful, loving reunion. That won't happen. True forgiveness is something that happens between you and the child in you. It means the child is no longer afraid of being hurt or abandoned. He knows he can count on your adult to love and protect him. He doesn't have to pretend to be your parent's parent; he can be a child. Someone is looking after him now. Once you know that your parents no longer have the power to hurt you, then you can begin to forgive.

"I had trouble with that word, *forgive*," Steve says. "At first it seemed like a whitewash to me. I thought it meant I had to excuse everything my parents did, and I wasn't about to do that. What happened really happened, so I wasn't going to deny it all over again just to say, 'I love you, Mom and Dad.' "

Forgiveness isn't a whitewash or a new form of denial. It's your personal declaration of independence. It says:

- That you love and accept yourself for what you are
- That you will love others—including your alcoholic parent—in the same way
- That you would like to be loved in return, but you don't require it
- That the alcoholic's game is over, at least for you
- That you refuse to allow your parent—or anyone else—to hurt you
- That you don't want to punish your parent
- That you acknowledge the effect of your parent's

disease on his life, but you're not willing to let it contaminate yours

- That you will allow your parent to be responsible for his own life and well-being
- That you realize what happened in the past—and it's over
- That you're ready to share new, healthy relationships—including one with your parent—based on your awareness of your needs as a worthwhile human being
- That you will honor those needs in others
- That you don't feel compelled to control life anymore, but you're ready to explore it
- That you accept the possibility that others—including your parent—may not be willing to share this kind of a relationship with you
- That you will not be bound to anyone by your need for love
- That you have learned, from loving yourself, that love encourages personal growth, compassion, and self-respect
- That you will accept—and give—no substitute for the real thing

Loving Relationships

As you begin to sense your own worth as a human being, you'll form new relationships based on mutual regard. You'll ask yourself, "What's in this for me?" and "What can I give to this relationship without depriving myself?"—not only when a relationship begins, but as it develops and changes.

Ironically, the healthier you become, the less likely it is that you will succeed in having a relationship with your alcoholic parent. And that will hurt. But you now have a loving adult who knows how to heal your pain. You will recover. You will also find some parental qualities among your friends.

"I'm not always sure of myself," says Dr. Yvonne Kaye about her own recovery from an alcoholic family. "I have fears. I make mistakes, and sometimes I feel pretty depressed. But I don't seek out people who are emotionally unavailable to me anymore. I have people in my life now who support me when I need strength, people who can laugh with me and cry with me—and *listen* to me. I have friends who care enough about me to tell me when they think I'm doing something that isn't good for me, and they do it in a loving way. I have a healthy family now!"

Martin gets a lot of feedback from his children. "When I take them to a ballgame and see them having a great time, I think, *Gee, that's something I never could do when I was a kid.* It makes me feel so good to see them just enjoying themselves, that it's as if I'm a kid myself—only this time around, I'm really having a childhood."

Even the best kind of relationships don't happen overnight. Be patient with them, and with yourself. You have a lot to learn about loving and being loved, and you'll make mistakes. So will others. And you still have old habits and patterns to undo. But you know what forgiveness is now. You know what love is now. You're ready to go on with your life.

CHAPTER NINE

NEGOTIATING OUR DIFFERENCES

IF YOU'RE NOT a child of an alcoholic, you may wonder why it's so hard for us to have normal, healthy relationships. Why would anyone want to remain in a relationship that puts her down, denies her needs, deprives her of personal fulfillment, and outlaws her feelings? Why? Because it seems safer there.

Normal, healthy relationships are for grown-ups, for people who can give and take, respect each other's differences, and put up with a reasonable amount of imperfection. Grown-ups don't have to control or submit to each other in order to stay in a relationship. They know they won't always get along. They'll have differences, sometimes big ones. But they know how to handle them: They negotiate.

If an ACOA isn't in recovery, she's anything but grown-up. She hasn't had any experience relating to people who accept her as she is. She only knows how to fit into her alcoholic parent's endless game by trying to please him, continually failing, and then blaming herself for the failure. When she sees the way healthy people interact, she wants to run the other way. It's too threatening.

"My girlfriend's family was so normal, it felt weird being with them," Fran says. "One time when I was eating dinner there, her mother and father began to argue, and I got terrified. I kept waiting for her father to start beating her mother, but it never happened. Later, when I went into the kitchen for something, I found them kissing each other. I never saw that in my house.

"A few years later, when my father got sick, my mother sent me to live with my brother and his wife, and that was a revelation. We *did* things! They had friends, and they'd go places with them. In the summer we'd go to the beach. At least once a week we went to a restaurant—that was the first time in my life I ever ate out. My father never wanted to go anywhere. He didn't want to leave his bottle.

"Things like that—my girlfriend and my brother's family—they showed me that some people didn't live the way we did. That made me want to be like them when I grew up."

Please Don't Disagree

It's said that ACOAs have to guess at what normal is. We're told that we think our family is the only one that is constantly in a state of war and that other families get along beautifully. When we discover that other people sometimes disagree, get angry, and even yell at each other, we become confused and disappointed.

The truth is that we're far more aware of the way healthy people live. We know what normal is. We just don't know to deal with it.

Elizabeth recalls that her childhood friends "were from families where someone had a drinking problem. I knew other kinds of kids, but I wasn't comfortable with them. I didn't how to talk to them.

"My best girlfriend's father was an alcoholic and so was mine. Maybe that's why we were so close. We used to go for long walks after school, and I could say to her, 'This is one of my dirty days,' and she knew what I meant. A 'dirty day' was usually a day after my father got drunk, and I'd be feeling very depressed because I hated him. But there were some kids I'd never be able to tell that to. Actually I didn't want to tell it to anybody, not even my best friend. But I knew she understood how I felt, and it was good just to be able to say I was having a dirty day."

"I watched a lot of TV when I was a kid," Martin says. "My favorite shows were family sitcoms like 'Father Knows Best' and 'The Ozzie and Harriet Show,' and I'd pretend the parents were my parents. I knew they weren't real, but that was as close as I could get to the kind of parents I wanted to have. I knew I couldn't fit in with people who were okay."

When I was a child, I knew there was another kind of world beyond the one where I lived. Some of my friends' parents didn't drink or argue or do crazy things, at least not while I was around. Some of them seemed to behave the way I thought parents should—that is, they seemed to know what they were doing. They even had enough know-how to help their children figure out what they were doing.

The odd thing is, I was afraid of people who knew what they were doing. They were spontaneous and therefore unpredictable. They were hard to read, so I couldn't always tell what they expected of me. I *knew* healthy people could argue with each other—but *I* didn't know how to argue with them. I *knew* healthy people didn't always approve of each other—but *I* was afraid to disapprove of them. I *understood* that people could look at life in different ways and still get along well—but *I* didn't know how to reconcile differences. I didn't have any experience in peaceful negotiations. My family always went in for the kill.

Trying to relate to people by pleasing them and

winning their approval seemed safer to me on two counts: It kept them from attacking me—and it kept me from attacking them. I was afraid of either outcome, but I didn't know any other way for people to resolve their differences. My history of relationships outside my family wasn't good: I was always afraid that someone might disagree with me—and I tried to demolish anyone who did.

When I met someone I liked, I looked for ways to make that person like me. I looked for areas of agreement—mutual interests, similar opinions, compatible values. But please note: I was not looking for things we both had in common. Far from it. I wanted to know what the other person liked, so I could persuade myself to like it, too. I didn't pretend to like it; I plunged into complete and wholehearted devotion to whatever was important to the other person. I behaved exactly the way I behaved with my alcoholic parents, which may seem like a strange thing for me to have done because my relationship with them was anything but successful. But at least it was predictable. I knew I would fail, and I was accustomed to failure. I knew I could survive it. Spontaneous, give-and-take behavior offered no such guarantee. Having no experience with it, I didn't know what my chances of survival were.

Survival is crucial to the children of alcoholic parents, because the threats to our lives were many and serious. We grew up in a war zone where our physical well-being and our sanity were always in danger. We were often exposed to attack by people who didn't know the meaning of restraint. But the worst threat of all was a form of spiritual death: We were forbidden to think for ourselves. Consequently something as minor as a difference of opinion can create terror in us. We expect to be attacked for it—because we *were* attacked.

Strike First

It's not uncommon today for ACOAs to be accused of exaggerating their childhood experiences. We have also been accused of blaming all our problems on our parents. Now that we are finally admitting the truth about our families, a lot people don't want to hear it. The effect can be similar to that of a "gaper-lock," where drivers slow down to get a good look at an accident and then turn away with a shudder.

At times I accuse myself of exaggerating. I've asked myself, *Did such things actually happen, and did they happen so often?* It's especially difficult for me to answer yes when I'm having a pleasant visit with my stepfather, a man who likes underdogs, brings flowers when he's invited to dinner, and still gets calls from people who worked with him before he retired. And then something will happen to assure me that my memory is indeed accurate.

For instance, not long ago my stepfather told me that a distant relative had died. It was a woman he and my mother had always despised, and he announced her death with glee. Then he began to reminisce. I never learned why the woman was the object of such hatred, because her transgressions seemed so minor, but I was shaken by the force of it. It reminded me of some other unwitting objects of my parents' hostility—political figures, celebrities, neighbors, former friends, and drinking buddies—people anyone might, for one reason or another, dislike, but not *hate*. I remembered, too, how I used to fear becoming the target of that hatred. I sensed it would settle for nothing less than my destruction.

It took very little to arouse this hatred. Sometimes I didn't even have to express a different opinion; sometimes my own point of view was enough. Depending on their mood, my parents could quickly distort or misinterpret almost anything I said, making it appear that I didn't approve of them. They knew how I felt about their drinking and it enraged them, but we couldn't talk about it openly because they denied there was a problem. So perhaps they looked for other opportunities to let me know how angry they were.

"Did you have a good time?" my stepfather might ask when I came home after spending a night with a friend.

"Yes," I might say.

"What are Lois's parents like?" my mother might ask.

"Nice," I might say.

"They're teachers, aren't they?" my stepfather might ask.

"Yes, both of them," I might say.

"Yes-s-s, of course," my mother might say. "And naturally you felt more comfortable with them than you do with us, didn't you? You like being with intellectuals. They're more your type, aren't they?"

I knew what was coming, but I felt helpless to stop it. "They're just teachers, Mom. Nothing special."

"Do they drink?"

"A little."

"Very straight and proper, aren't they? And you like that, don't you? Did you tell them about us and how terrible we are? Did you go into your act and tell them that we're always drunk?"

On and on it would go until I ran to my room for shelter, with my mother pursuing me and screaming at me outside my door. Somehow that door seemed such a flimsy barricade between me and so much fury. I felt as if it might give way at any moment, and I would be crushed by what was on the other side of it. My parents' rage was so intense, so far out of proportion to what was really happening, that it threatened to exterminate me.

At the slightest sign of disagreement in anyone else, I used to expect the same thing to happen, even though I could see that other people didn't always react so violently. In a typical attitude of self-blame, I thought I might provoke that response in anyone. And I had reason to think that was true, because very often I sought relationships with people who behaved like my parents and were ready to attack. But even if they didn't, my fear almost paralyzed me. I felt so vulnerable that I wanted to run and hide, but I couldn't move. Besides, I didn't know where to go. There seemed to be no one I could call on to help me withstand the coming attack.

Therefore, *I* attacked. It was a matter of striking first, before I was struck down. I used the weapons my parents used: distortion, misinterpretation, accusation. I learned to use language like a sword. I fought savagely over the most trivial things—anything to prove that if you disagreed with me, *you* were wrong and deserved to be attacked, anything to avoid feeling that *I* was wrong.

Every time I hurt someone, I suffered my parents' kind of remorse, and that only increased my fear. Was I becoming like them? Yes. Did I have to? Absolutely not.

As long as I allowed my overburdened, frightened child to control my relationships with other people, I could count on one of two results: I would give in to people who wanted to play games, or I would defend myself against people who had no intention of attacking me. It was time to let my adult take over.

Making Space for Disagreements

"If he's going to recover, an adult child of an alcoholic has to learn how to validate himself," says Vincent DiPascuale. "For a long time he's been around people who've been telling him what they want him to be, but now he has to get a real sense of who he is. He has to begin to make his own rules in life, based on the kind of person he is. He has to begin to appreciate his own beautiful self. And he's going to pay a price for that, because a lot of the people he knows aren't going to like what he's doing. Some of them will say, 'Oh, now look what you've done! I can't understand what's happened to you, you used to be such a nice person, but now you're messing up everything.' When the adult child begins to get healthy, he's going to get criticized, but as a friend of mine remarked, 'You know you're recovering when people start talking about you.' "

At various times in our recovery, it's a good idea to take time out to practice on ourselves before going out into the world to do something we haven't been able to do before. As Yvonne Kaye says, "One reason why you have to love yourself first before you can love someone else is that it's the only way you learn how love feels. You learn what love is, and then, when you want to give it to someone else, you know *what* you want to give. Love isn't just a word. It's something you have to experience directly—by loving yourself."

So it is with our relationships. Before we can improve the way we interact with people, we have to make some changes within ourselves. Even if we know what normal is, we still have to learn how to *be* normal. We can't ask anyone to accept us as we are until we accept ourselves. We can't respect anyone else's beautiful self until we appreciate our own. We can't put up with anyone else's imperfections until we have lived with our own. We can't negotiate our differences with others until we hammer out our own agreement with ourselves.

When the child and the adult in me made contact, I thought what any ACOA would think: that they would get along fine as long as the child behaved herself and didn't do anything wrong. I honestly didn't expect the relationship to last, because sooner or later the child would do something the adult didn't like. In time she did. But the adult didn't attack, didn't even criticize. The adult just came right out and said, "Hey, you goofed!" She didn't go away. She didn't withdraw her love. From that experience, I began to understand what nurture means: I can love someone and not like something he does—and I can let him know it.

There are several ways in which the child in me is different from my adult: The child is easily distracted and the adult likes to get a job done; the child laughs at some things the adult takes seriously; the child is impatient and the adult forgets to take time out; the child is very sensitive and the adult can put feelings aside; the child is reckless and the adult is aware of danger. The two of them don't always want to go in the same direction, at the same time, or at the same pace. But they get along. They value each other's distinctiveness. They respect each other's right to be herself. It was their regard for each other that gave me some guidelines for dealing with differences in my relationships with others:

- There is nothing wrong with being different, so there is no reason to attack or to fear being attacked.
- We can disagree comfortably instead of aggressively; we can make some space for our differences to fit into our relationship instead of trying to stamp them out.
- We can ignore some of our differences, especially if they are unimportant.
- We can express disapproval of our differences without disapproving of each other.
- We can respect each other's points of view; we

don't have to change, or try to make each other change.

- We can negotiate our differences *only* if we don't feel like helpless children who are afraid we'll be attacked if we dare to think for ourselves. When we allow our adult to take charge of our relationships, we don't have to be afraid. Our adult can defend us if the need arises, and very often it won't, so we don't have to be ready to strike first. In fact, we can sit back, be ourselves, be different, state our points of view, and even disagree in an absolutely nonthreatening manner.
- We can stop looking at ourselves through the eyes of our alcoholic parents, seeking out openings for attack. Instead we can look at ourselves and others through our own adult eyes. We can see what's good and what's not so good, what needs help and what has to be accepted.

When we're able to negotiate our differences, we know we've come a long way toward maturity. We're saying that it's safe for me to be me and you to be you—and normally we'll get along.

CHAPTER TEN

PROVIDING
FOR OURSELVES

THE CHILDREN OF alcoholic parents don't know how to be good to themselves. They only know how to make sacrifices—and resent them. That is not an unusual cause-and-effect. Nobody likes to make sacrifices, and certainly not when it becomes a way of life.

Rachel is beginning to realize that a twelve-hour day is too long to work, especially without overtime pay. "But my boss isn't the kind you can talk to," she says. "Mention money, and he starts yelling. I can't take that. I suppose I ought to look for a better job, but I've put in a lot of years here. I think they owe me something."

Martin insists that he doesn't regret the hardships of his childhood. "I'm sure they made me a better person," he says. But many ACOAs would disagree with him. They feel they've been cheated, not only by their alcoholic parents but by everyone they ever loved, and they don't mind letting people know it.

Marian is bitter about her personal situation. Her divorce could soon become final, and her husband wants to marry again, but Marian is delaying the decree by demanding changes in the settlement agreement. "I never asked for anything while we were married," she says, "and now it's time I did."

Contrary to many studies that characterize ACOAs

as approval-seekers, there is a flip side to that part of us, too. Rub us the wrong way, and you'll get sparks.

"The first time I attended a conference of ACOAs, I was shocked," says Dr. Yvonne Kaye. "They were the rudest, most self-pitying *brats* I'd ever met in my life!" She went on to work with many of them successfully, but she encourages them to stop seeing themselves as victims. "It's a terrible way they grew up, and I understand it because the same thing happened to me. I come from a home where there was always shouting and cursing. I don't mean only curse *words*; people always think curse words are terrible, but there are worse kinds of words. *Stupid, dumb, you fool*—those are the real curse words. They're the ones that do the damage. But you have to let those things go. When one of my patients keeps telling me how rotten her parents were, I say, 'Don't tell me any more about what you suffered—tell me what you're going to do about it. I don't want to know anymore about the past. Tell me about right now. What are you going to do for yourself *right now?*' "

Steve says he went through a long period of "brathood." It began when he confronted the truth about his alcoholic parents. "I felt sorry for myself. When I saw kids having a good time, I felt like crying because I didn't have a childhood. I felt like 'poor Steve.' I wanted to get something back for all the things I missed. I wanted some pity. But, hell, if you didn't have a good childhood, tough. You have to move on from there."

"We treat ACOAs with love and respect," says Mary Hoffman of Caron Counseling Services. "We know that bad behavior, in their situation, is really a defense. It's something they had to learn how to do in order to survive in their family of origin."

Sacrifice Can Become a Habit

To this day I have a hard time buying myself an ice cream cone. I no longer feel guilty about a lot of other things I buy for myself, but an ice cream cone has a special significance in my memory. When I was growing up, an ice cream cone was a small, inexpensive luxury that almost everyone took for granted. But on the way home from school, when my friends stopped at the ice cream store for a cone, I didn't buy one. I used to say I didn't like ice cream, but that wasn't true. I took a certain measure of pride in denying myself something I enjoyed and wanted very much. I think I was trying to need less to cover up the fact that my parents gave me so little. It didn't work. It couldn't possibly. Nor could all the other, larger sacrifices I made, not only in material things but emotionally. Nevertheless I had to keep trying. ACOAs are very persistent; we don't see alternatives or options. We see only the way our alcoholic parent has laid out for us, and we don't dare depart from it.

Even after we're grown up, wanting something makes us uncomfortable. We feel selfish and guilty, as if, by giving something to ourselves, we're taking something away from our parent. We put off buying what we need because it makes us feel greedy, or sometimes we'll do just the opposite and buy things impulsively, quickly, before we can stop ourselves. That's how we try to avoid our guilt, but of course we don't succeed. The guilt is even worse because in our haste we probably bought more than we absolutely needed, and we don't know how to forgive ourselves. Be assured, we take no pleasure in these splurges.

We do take pleasure in saying no to ourselves. It makes us feel like good people, as if by taking less for ourselves, we make it possible for someone—our parent, or any one of a number of stand-ins—to have more. Self-deprivation can become such a habit that it seems almost easy.

It's much harder for ACOAs to provide for ourselves: to see that we are paid what we're worth for the work we do; to work hard enough and well enough to get a promotion and a better income; to dress well or to own more than the clothes we actually need; to rest when we're tired; to take care of our health and pay attention to our emotional needs. We feel wrong when we want some of the better things in life, and it doesn't occur to us to make it our business to earn them. Oh, we'll work hard and we'll get ahead, but not to satisfy ourselves and add some pleasure to our lives. We'll work hard for praise and approval, for the promise that we'll be looked after by whoever supervises us. We'll slave for peanuts and then resent being hungry. Many of us are out of touch with our tastes and preferences because we don't feel they're important. Ask us where we'd like to go or what we'd like to do, and we'll answer, "Whatever you like is fine with me." And if it isn't, we'll resent you for not being able to read our mind, but you'll never hear it from us.

We don't know what to do with our resentment. It was always something we hid because it made us feel as if we didn't love our parents, and we *had* to love our parents. So the resentment builds up inside of us, generating a lot of heat, and it comes out in the form of emotional steam. We begin to resent people who have what we don't have. We begin to begrudge others the satisfaction of their needs. We can't relate to people we consider more fortunate than we are. We want them to fail, to be deprived of something they want and, sometimes, if we can deprive them, we do. We're not happy about some of the things we do, but we can't always undo them. What's worse, we realize that we're responding to people the way our parents responded to us: We're blaming them for our unhappiness.

If we want to change, to break this pattern of self-deprivation and resentment, we can. The remedy is to see ourselves as competent, worthwhile adults who can provide for our own needs, and not as helpless, undeserving children making do with crumbs of satisfaction left over from other people's feasts. But this change will be an especially difficult part of our recovery—because in this area many of the programs intended to help us are actually working in the opposite direction.

Obstacles to Recovery

Ironically, unintentionally, and unfortunately, many recovery programs preach that ACOAs are not victims, yet at the same time they encourage us to behave like victims. They advise us not to blame our parents for being alcoholics, yet they tell us we are helpless to do anything about alcoholism. The result is that we feel as if we are part of the alcoholic's problems, perhaps even the cause of them. We feel as if we are trapped in a maze we didn't create or choose to enter, yet supposedly there is no way out. Is it any wonder that some of us feel sorry for ourselves? Or that some of us are rude and touchy?

If we have come this far, if we are trying to recover from the emotional handicaps of growing up with an alcoholic parent, then we don't want to be treated like alcoholics. Some of our problems may at times appear to be similar to those of the alcoholic, but their causes are different. We didn't choose to be born, and in our earliest years we were unable to defend ourselves against the abuses of a parent. In that sense we *were* victims and we *were* helpless against alcoholism. But neither of those conditions is true now, and this is what we must begin to realize if we are to recover completely. We do not have to *remain* victims, and there are *many* things we can do to overcome the effects of alcoholism on our own lives. But first things first: Painful as it is to us, and disturbing as it may be to our parents, we must revisit the trauma of our past and acknowledge ourselves as victims before we can stop being victims in the present. We have to see what happened to us before we can change the effect it had on us.

By far, most recovery programs for ACOAs—from no-cost, self-help groups to more costly live-in and facilitated programs—are founded on The Twelve Steps, a program developed for alcoholics by the founders of Alcoholics Anonymous. These Steps, originally intended for male alcoholics, are still read aloud at the beginning of AA meetings. Now, however, a reading of these same Steps also begins the ACOA meetings sponsored by Al-Anon and many other recovery programs:

1. We admitted we were powerless over alcohol— that our lives had become unmanageable.
2. Came to believe that a Power greater than ourselves could restore us to sanity.
3. Made a decision to turn our will and our lives over to the care of God as we understood Him.
4. Made a searching and fearless moral inventory of ourselves.
5. Admitted to God, to ourselves and to another human being the exact nature of our wrongs.
6. Were entirely ready to have God remove all these defects of character.
7. Humbly asked Him to remove our shortcomings.

8. Made a list of all persons we had harmed and became willing to make amends to them all.

9. Made direct amends to such people wherever possible except when to do so would injure them or others.

10. Continued to take personal inventory and when we were wrong promptly admitted it.

11. Sought through prayer and meditation to improve our conscious contact with God as we understood Him, praying only for knowledge of His will for us and the power to carry that out.

12. Having had a spiritual awakening as the result of these Steps, we tried to carry this message to others, and to practice these principles in all our affairs.

There is nothing in these Twelve Steps about loving the self—and others. There is a great deal of guilt, remorse, humility, confession, dependence, repentance, and restitution, but nothing about healing the past and building a healthy future. The penitent attitude of The Twelve Steps may be what the recovering alcoholic needs, but to the child of the alcoholic they repeat and confirm what he has heard all his life: *It's your fault—make it up to me.* Of course, the child embraces The Steps; they are his second nature. Self-esteem, independence, and personal growth remain alien to him because they conflict with the attitude of helplessness The Twelve Steps promote. Nor do The Steps offer him an opportunity to examine, understand, and express his own feelings. Instead he is urged to tally up his wrongdoings, proclaim them, and then atone for them.

Another disturbing aspect of AA's philosophy about the recovery of children of alcoholics is that it is alcoholic-centered. Instead of learning how to focus his attention on himself and his own needs, the ACOA spends most of his time developing specific responses to the alcoholic's behavior patterns. He learns to accept alcoholism as a disease over which the alcoholic has no control, he avoids "dumping" on his alcoholic parent and practices ways to detach himself from involvement in his parent's alcoholic behavior. Thus the alcoholic parent and the game he plays remain a powerful presence in the life of the child.

Sitting in on some Al-Anon-sponsored self-help groups for ACOAs, I was distressed by the depression and self-accusation that permeated the environment week after week. I could accept it in men and women who were new to recovery programs, but not in those (and there were many) who had been in a program for years.

"I don't know why they insist on using the AA program for ACOAs, because the ACOA is not the same as the alcoholic," says Dr. Jean Kirkpatrick, founder of Women for Sobriety, a recovery program for women alcoholics. "There are so many contradictions in that approach. The language of The Twelve Step program is very negative: helplessness, humility, turn-yourself-over-to-a-Higher-Power—that's all dependency, dependency, dependency!"

Women for Sobriety does not yet offer a recovery program for the children of alcoholics, but much of its founder's philosophy applies to ACOAs. She has rewritten the original Twelve Steps—and added one—to express her conviction that self-discovery and self-esteem are essential to recovery:

1. I have a drinking (life-threatening) problem that once had me.
2. Negative emotions destroy only myself.
3. Happiness is a habit I will develop.
4. Problems bother me only to the degree I permit them to.

5. I am what I think.
6. Life can be ordinary or it can be great.
7. Love can change the course of my world.
8. The fundamental object of life is emotional and spiritual growth.
9. The past is gone forever.
10. All love given returns twofold.
11. Enthusiasm is my daily exercise.
12. I am a competent woman and have much to give life.
13. I am responsible for myself and for my actions.

"In the beginning AA or Al-Anon is effective because it's good to be with people who have the same problem you do," Dr. Kirkpatrick advises, "but only in the *very* beginning—before you become addicted to the meetings themselves."

I had wondered about that. I had noticed how compulsively some members cling to the meetings, lingering on in the room and then in the parking lot, leaving only when the lights are turned off. And at the next week's meeting, you can tell from bits of conversations that some of the group have phoned each other frequently. There seems to be nothing else going on in their lives except "the program"—and being an ACOA.

Dr. Jean Kirkpatrick is a recovering alcoholic. "I made AA my life," she says, "and as long as it was, I stayed sober. But I could not live without that 'shot.' It took the place of alcohol. So I left AA because I didn't think it was good for me to be dependent on anything. Now I always say, if you keep going to AA, you're going to become a professional alcoholic. You'll go to a party, you'll announce, 'I'm an alcoholic,' and you'll expect everybody to drop dead! The label becomes your identity rather than your illness. And it's the same with an ACOA. Sure, you're the child of an alcoholic, but there are other facets in your life. Being the child of an alcoholic is part of your emotional response to life, and it affects some other parts of you as well—but you're a lot more than just an ACOA."

Vincent DiPascuale's Starting Point program encourages ACOAs to form relationships "with all kinds of people. That's essential to recovery, but when you do that, you may have to leave some of your friends behind. Some of them won't want to go that far with you. Sure, they'll wish you luck and they may even give you a send-off party, but privately they'll think you're nuts to go on by yourself."

At Caron's Counseling Services, ACOAs are advised to participate in aftercare groups and to seek counseling for six months to a year after completing the five-and-a-half-day Caron program. Mary Hoffman says, "We don't advise anyone to stay in aftercare for more than a year. Then it's time for them to go out into the world and practice what they've learned. It's important to become independent."

In the ACOA groups sponsored by AA's Al-Anon, the emphasis is quite different. At the end of each meeting, members hold hands and stand in a circle while they recite the Lord's Prayer. "Keep coming back," they say to each other. "It really works!" To most of the members, participation in the group is for life, and those who express optimism about their progress are quickly reminded that it was their attendance at the meetings that made it possible.

Dr. Claude Steiner sees this unending program as fitting into the alcoholic's game: "The therapist who insists on the need to continue treatment when a patient has given up his script is playing the role of the Persecutor as well. This persecutory role is also often played by individuals in AA ('Once an alcoholic always an alcoholic') and other self-help organizations." As far as the ACOA is concerned, it may only reinforce his feelings of dependency and keep the game going.

"They can't seem to get it through their heads that people can do things for themselves—that after a while they *should* do things for themselves," says Dr. Kirkpatrick.

Karen Schulte, M.S.W., a therapist in the field of alcohol dependency, approaches the subject from another angle. "It's true that AA replaces one rigid, compulsive behavior with another, The Twelve Steps. The group does become a way of life for each member, and that may be why it works in the early stages of recovery. But recovery is many different stages, and some people get stuck along the way. Some are able to grow and leave their meetings. But many never grow that far. They are the ones who are likely to stay in AA or Al-Anon groups for life.

"These people remind me of my daughter when she was about six years old. One day we had a disagreement and she said she was going to leave home. I held my breath while I watched her put some clothes in a suitcase. Then I watched her walk up the driveway toward the street, knowing I couldn't let her go much farther on her own. When she approached the curb, she stopped and stood there for a few minutes. Then she turned around and slowly walked back to the house. 'I'm too little,' she said when she came inside. 'I can't even cross the street.' That's the way a lot of recovering alcoholics feel about leaving the group.

"I agree with several of the criticisms of AA. But then I remember that AA was there for the alcoholic when no one else was. Yet there is a population at risk in this country that does have to be considered, and they aren't being reached by AA's methods. This is especially true of the children of alcoholics, and they weren't even part of the picture back in the days when AA began. But it doesn't seem valid to apply the same standards to the children of alcoholics, and this is what The Twelve Steps do. The children of alcoholics aren't the same as alcoholics. Children don't have choices—they're victims, and that's a problem in itself. The alcoholic parent may not be a functioning adult, but he or she is at least a biological adult, and that implies choices."

Be Good to Yourself

I had to stop trying to make my parents love me before I could begin to appreciate my own value as a person. I had to stop looking at myself through my parents' eyes and discover myself through the eyes of my adult. In other words, I had to stop being my parents' child and become my own child.

There *is* something we all can do about the effect of alcoholism on our own lives. We can give the child in us a normal, healthy life. It took time, but gradually I began to realize that I had a right to be happy. I didn't have to stay trapped in the maze of the past, and indeed there is a way out. I had to find it for myself by asserting my right to a life based on my own needs and preferences rather than those of my alcoholic parents.

Breaking the pattern of self-deprivation takes time and practice in being good to yourself. It helps to follow a few simple rules:

When you want something, ask your adult for it. It's normal for a child to have needs, and it's normal for a parent to want the child to enjoy life. You weren't a normal child and you didn't have normal parents, but things are different now. You're becoming a healthy child because you have a healthy adult for a parent. And healthy parents are happy when their children are happy. So go ahead—ask for what you want. You're worth it. If it's more than your adult can give you, at least you'll know that's the reason. Maybe the two of you can figure out how to get what you want. And if you can't, you'll still have each other.

Ask yourself, What's in this for me? Are you giving too much to your relationships? Are you getting anything back? If you're not, if you're caught up in someone's game and feel guilty about pulling out of it, let your adult take over and do it for you.

Recently I went to dinner with someone I hadn't seen for almost a year. The truth is, I had been avoiding her because I was becoming impatient with her. She had a lot of problems and wasn't doing anything to solve them, yet she constantly asked for advice and never took it. I accused myself of treating her unfairly. After all, I said to myself, what did it cost me to listen to her complaints and give her the sympathy she obviously wanted from me? I made up my mind that when I saw her again I would try to make her feel good. I wouldn't talk about anything that might cause us to disagree. I would control my impatience. We would have a lovely evening.

And it was not lovely at all. My friend and I were genuinely glad to see each other, but the glow faded very quickly. Halfway through dinner I began wishing I were home. I was hearing the same old complaints about other people getting all the breaks in life, and I could feel myself being pulled into—you guessed it!—a game! I thought I was beyond such things, but apparently I wasn't. My adult, however, is, and my view of the situation through her eyes was entirely different.

Almost immediately I realized why I was uncomfortable: My child had needs, and I was ignoring them. I was in a sacrificial relationship that asked a great deal of me and gave nothing back. My child didn't want to be used as a shoulder to cry on. She didn't want to be treated like a pretend mother. She wanted a genuine, give-and-take interaction. She needed a different kind of friend.

As soon as my adult got my child out of the game, I felt better. I could relax and let my friend complain. When she asked for advice, I answered honestly: I didn't have any—what did *she* think she ought to do? My friend didn't like my answer, and I don't know what will happen to our relationship. But unless there is something in it for me, it really isn't a relationship. It's a game I don't want to play.

Stop putting yourself down. "The children of alcoholics put themselves down so much, and they don't even realize it," says Dr. Yvonne Kaye. "Very often they'll start to ask me a question by saying, 'This is probably a dumb question . . . ,' or 'I know this sounds stupid . . .' When that happens, I say to them, 'Look, if it's a dumb question, then I don't want to hear it,' or 'If it's stupid, why are you asking it?' I'm trying to help them realize how unfair they are to themselves."

Dr. Kaye also gives her patients some homework. "I ask them to carry a card around with them and to mark down each time they say something derogatory about themselves—whether they say it out loud or in their mind. One man told me, 'Well, I won't have any marks on my card next week because I don't do things like that.' 'Then what the hell are you doing here?' I asked him. 'Because either you're up to your eyeballs in denial or you're in such good shape, you don't need to be here at all!' "

How often do you put yourself down? Probably a lot more than you realize. Start checking up on yourself. If you don't like the way you're treating yourself, that's a healthy sign of recovery. Make some changes.

Start building yourself up. After Fran broke up with the young man who "used her for a doormat," she gave up a promising job and moved to be near a childhood friend. "This was someone who always thought a lot of me, and that's what I needed at that time. I was at a very low point in my life. I thought there wasn't anything worthwhile about me, and I guess I was sort of daring my friend to agree with me. But she didn't. I could see right away that her opinion of me hadn't changed, and I began to feel better about myself. After living in that kind of atmosphere for a few months, I began to see myself as a really good person. I felt I could do just about anything I put my mind to. That's when I stopped going to singles bars to meet people. I put more effort into getting a job that could lead to something better. Even the friends I made were different. They really cared about me."

Dr. Kaye calls it "acting as if." If you don't think you're worth much, then try behaving *as if* you are. Do what a worthwhile person would do. Pretty soon you may realize that you *are* one.

Go for what you want. Is there something you've always wanted to do, someplace you've always wanted to go, something you've always wanted to become? And did you always deny yourself because you thought your parent wouldn't approve? Well, you don't have to try to please your parent anymore. By now you know it never was, and never will be, possible. But you can please yourself.

Don't expect everyone to agree with your decision. Some people won't like it, but that's life.

The first step Sara took toward resuming her career was to join a local chapter of a professional women's organization. "My husband was the one who encouraged me, and that was great. Working in the organization built up my self-confidence because I discovered what a good organizer I am. I decided to go back to teaching part time because I realized I could handle it and still look after my family. Of course, we had to make some adjustments because I didn't have time to do everything I used to do. But that was all right. Then my organization named me to represent them at a national convention, which meant I would be away for a couple of days. I couldn't believe the way my husband reacted to that! On the morning I was leaving, he got this helpless look on his face and said, 'Gee, what are we going to eat while you're away?'

"For a moment I had that old twinge of guilt, but only for a moment. 'Dog food!' I said. 'What the hell do I care what you eat? I'm leaving!' And I went to my car, got in, and drove off. I had a damned good time at the convention, too.

"I know some people who give up rather than go through that crap. But I fight against that kind of bondage."

Steve has a thriving business, but he's going to start working only three days a week because he plans to go to law school. "I always wanted to be a lawyer, but I found a million reasons not to do it. None of them were mine. It was my father's voice I kept hearing, saying, 'No, you'll never make it.' It took a long time for me to get his voice out of my head so I could hear my own. And I was saying something really different. I was saying, 'Sure, go for it. What have you got to lose?' "

You've got the best reason in the world to be good to yourself: You're a valuable person.

CHAPTER ELEVEN

SAFETY FIRST

DURING THE PAST ten years Desmond has had six jobs. Twice his department was reduced and he was let go; three times he was fired. "I really want to hold on to this one," he says of his present job. "I'm not getting any younger."

Desmond's father was an alcoholic and a hard man to please. "He could find fault with anything," Desmond says. "I can't remember him ever giving my brother or me a word of praise when we were growing up. He wanted us to be the best at everything—Olympic athletes, geniuses, Most-Likely-to-Succeed and Most Popular. We couldn't even get close to one of them!

"I thought my father was a very successful man. He went into his father's business right out of college. They manufactured shoes. It was a small company, but they did all right. I never knew exactly what my father did there, but he had a fancy title and he brought home good money. We lived well.

"When it was time for my brother and me to go into the business, there wasn't anything left. My grandfather had died, and I guess my father really didn't do such a good job running things because the company went bankrupt the year my brother graduated from college. My father blamed it on all the imports coming into the country, and a lot of shoe companies went under because of that. But I think his company was in trouble before that happened. Anyway, my father came out of it with enough money to live on. He never tried to get another job. He said he was too old to start over. Only young guys could do that, he said. Then he'd tell us to go out and swing the world by the tail."

Desmond is beginning to understand why he lost one job after another. "I was imitating my father," he says. "I thought he was Mr. Success, and I was trying to copy him. I was always looking for imperfections and pointing my finger at them. Instead of doing my job and minding my own business, I'd go around telling everyone what they were doing wrong. I'd even tell my boss how to run the department. It was crazy!"

The same thing kept happening, job after job. Capable as Desmond was, his employers eventually gave up on him. "I saw myself as a reformer, but to everyone else I was a pain in the butt," he says.

Didn't he realize he was making the same mistake over and over?

"Yes," he says. "But I had to keep doing it. I was afraid to try anything different. I know this sounds crazy, but I was afraid I'd fail."

Change Is Scary

It is said that ACOAs don't take risks. But we do, all the time. The way we live is a tremendous risk in itself: We would almost rather die than change; we self-destruct: we're afraid to fail and afraid to succeed.

Desmond says he usually could see the end coming. "My boss would call me into his office for a friendly chat. He'd suggest that maybe I could be more of a team player. I'd sit there and say, 'Sure, sure, I understand, thanks, you've been a real help.' I knew what he was talking about because I saw other people doing it. But me? I didn't know how to be a team player. I only knew how to try pleasing my father, and that sure didn't work. So the only other thing I knew was being *like* my father—even though it meant there would be another chat in the boss's office and I'd be let go.

"When I lost a job, it was my family who suffered the most, but I wasn't thinking about them. All I thought about was my father, and what he would say. And he'd always say the same thing: 'I knew it was going to happen.' In a way, it was a relief to get fired, because it made my father right. Crazy, isn't it?"

Looking back to that time, Desmond can see that, as frightening as it was to get fired, he was even more afraid to try to do his job well. "For two reasons," he says. "First, it would have meant doing something different—and not knowing what was going to happen as a result. I knew how to deal with losing a job because I'd been there so often before. It was grim, but I knew I'd survive. Suppose I didn't get fired? Suppose I even got a promotion or a pat on the back? What might happen next? Would I come up against something I couldn't handle? Would I make an even bigger fool of myself? The possibility of success presented me with an awful lot of uncertainties.

"My other fear was my father. He liked being the big shot. I didn't want to make him think he wasn't. It's still hard for me to go all out for anything. I'm afraid that if I get what I want, I'll lose my father. I'm not up to that. At least, not yet."

Desmond is typical of so many ACOAs who perceive their problems intellectually. We know what's wrong, we know what to do, but we can't seem to do it. Why not? Why is it so hard for us to change for the better?

Here, again, is an example of the way our hurt child can influence our behavior. Change is always a risky business. It means we have to assess new situations, process new information, consider options, and make decisions. Sometimes we have to do it all within seconds. It's not a task a child can handle, and it's not surprising that a child would shrink from it. Children need consistency and security. Changing is something for an adult to do.

If you want to change the way you behave, but you're afraid something terrible will happen if you do, you may have to take some time out from your immediate problems and attend to your child. He's the one who's trembling. Listen to his fears. Let him know you're there to take care of him. Assure him of your love and protection. Then leave him in a safe place with something a child likes to do—while your adult rearranges your life to suit your needs.

Growing Up with Danger

ACOAs have no sense of safety. Our disregard for our own well-being sometimes enables us to achieve what many people wouldn't even attempt, and this is a characteristic that attracts a lot of attention. But more often we self-destruct. We go full-steam-ahead toward a goal; then we either leap off the train just before we get there, or we derail.

If we seem to be unaware of danger, it's because we're accustomed to it. We grew up with it. As children, we lived in an atmosphere of constant, imminent danger. We saw our parents jeopardizing themselves twenty-four hours a day, yet they often survived, or so we wanted to believe. We went along with them in denying that they failed, or that any damage was done. Now we think people can jump off moving trains without getting hurt. And we do it all the time. When we hurt ourselves, it's the same old story: We deny it or blame someone else.

The stereotype of the down-and-out alcoholic is misleading. Many more alcoholics hold down steady jobs and go on to retire with a pension. Many are never absent or late for work, and many are cited for dedicated service to an employer. That's what the world sees and what the world prizes. What the alcoholic's child sees are parents drinking themselves into a stupor, driving while drunk, getting into brawls and shouting matches, making fools of themselves in public and sometimes in front of their employers. The child sees his parents constantly risking the loss of their livelihood, their health, their security, and their reputation by the way they behave on their own time. Yet his parents are seldom penalized or held accountable for their behavior because, as Vincent DiPascuale pointed out, our culture values a steady job performance more than it values sobriety. It values job performance more than it values sober driving or rational thinking or the nurturing (rather than the abuse) of families.

ACOAs don't know what safety is because we weren't safe or secure as children. We were exposed to shame and abuse, to fear and rage by those who were supposed to protect us. Without realizing it, we lived precariously. When we grow up, we still don't try to protect ourselves because we don't think our safety and well-being are important. We haven't learned that the only safe way to get off a train is to wait until it stops. We don't cover our ass because our parents never did, and they insisted they were fine. In fact, they ridiculed people who were wiser and sober, and, like our parents, we developed a contempt for caution and self-protection. Now we're paying a price for winging it through life. We're always afraid—and we don't realize that we don't have to be.

I brought many childhood anxieties with me as I grew up. When I was supposedly an adult, I was afraid to be alone in my house at night. I knew why: as a child I woke up so often to find my parents gone, where and for how long I never knew. After I grew up, the darkness of an empty house, or even a room, made me feel completely helpless and abandoned. Finally I was able to understand that it was my child who was terrified. My adult could assess my situation and make reasonable provisions for my security, but that wasn't enough to satisfy my child. She needed something more. So I began to leave a night-light on in my bedroom. I still do. It's for my child. If she wakes up, she knows immediately that I'm right there.

For years after I learned to drive, I had a feeling of unwarranted terror when I got behind the wheel. Plenty of other people told me they enjoyed driving, but I never did. As I became more aware of my child, I realized that I was letting her fears affect my driving. When I was a little girl, I was often a passenger in a car driven by someone who was drunk. I knew the terror of speeding down the wrong side of a road late at night, of taking corners in a wild arc, of swerving uncertainly. And all the time I was too small to see over the dashboard or past the front seats. I could only hear and feel the absence of control, the presence of danger. I couldn't do anything about it, but I remember wanting to seize the wheel and stop the car. Many years later the child had to go through the same hell every time I got in the car.

It took a while, but eventually I was able to make driving a pleasant experience for both my adult and my child. I keep her up front beside me so that she can see where we're going and enjoy the scenery. By now she knows that I'm a reliable driver and that little children don't have to worry about such things.

The Threat of Success

Roy also had a hard time holding on to a job. He's an intelligent, talented, articulate man, the kind you'd expect to find on a fast track to the top. And he always started out that way. During his first year in his most recent job, he doubled the sales of heavy farm equipment in his territory. Then he was called into the office to explain some items on his expense account report, and he threw a punch at the accounts supervisor. End of job. Before that, he was top salesman of the year for another company but failed to show up at the awards presentation dinner. He left a message on the sales manager's answering machine saying he was quitting. No explanation offered.

"I sabotaged myself," Roy says. "As soon as I started doing well, I got scared. I just knew something terrible was going to happen—so I'd make it happen. That time with my expense account, I deliberately padded it. I knew they'd call me on it. I was looking for trouble because I wanted a way out."

A way out of what?

"Success," Roy says. "I wanted it, but I was afraid of it."

Many ACOAs are successful in the sense that they achieve what they set out to do, but few of them enjoy it. Many more avoid success and repeatedly invite failure.

To most of us, the payoff for success is not reward and satisfaction, but punishment and suffering. We remember being caught between our parents' demands for success and their jealousy of it. Instead of taking pride in our achievement, they took credit for it. Or they belittled it because it competed with their own claims to success. Instead of winning their approval, our achievement earned their contempt, resentment, and anger. They punished us for doing something right—because they always told us we were wrong.

Much later in life, success still presents the ACOA with a dilemma. We can't enjoy what we achieve because it disqualifies us for the alcoholic's game. It becomes a barrier to the parental love we want so desperately. Besides, we don't believe that success will last. We're convinced that sooner or later everybody will find out that we're not what we appear to be, and they'll take our success away.

So why not jump off the train before it gets to where it's going? Why not get off before somebody throws us off?

Love Is Our Best Protection

Children of alcoholics self-destruct because they don't love themselves. They don't love anyone except the alcoholic parent, or someone who behaves just like her. And when you don't love yourself, you don't care what happens to you.

You care very much what happens to your parent. You will suffer deprivation, pain, and humiliation without protest as long as you believe that in some way you are doing it for your parent. You don't feel your own injuries, but you feel your parent's slightest discomfort intensely. All your sensitivities and protectiveness are given over to her and you live through her. If you fail to make her happy, you may even lose your desire to live. Many ACOAs attempt suicide; many come close to it through the risks they take.

The last time Desmond lost a job he bought a bottle of liquor on the way home and then sat in the garage drinking, with the engine running. "I was lucky," he says, "because my wife came home early that day and found me before it was too late.

"When I came to in the hospital, it was the damnedest thing—I was *shocked* by what I tried to do! It was as if I had done it under hypnosis instead of consciously, as if something *made* me do it. I still can't believe that I tried to end my own life! But that's how little I cared about myself."

Desmond's realization motivated him to seek help. He has been in therapy for almost a year, and he is making some changes in the way he lives. "The most radical change I've made is that I'm trying to be myself instead of copying someone else," he says. "From one day to the next, I don't know what's going to happen, because being myself is a very new experience. But I'm actually beginning to enjoy it. I really like this person I am. He's an okay guy.

"Feeling better about myself makes it easier for me to get along with people. I'm still a picky person. I still think there's a better way to do almost anything. But I go about it in a different way. I don't belittle people. I try to *persuade* them that maybe there's a better way to do something."

Desmond still has a lot of recovery ahead of him. "Even though I'm feeling okay about who I am, I know I'm still not okay with my father. It's very hard for me to give up trying to please him."

At some point in our recovery, ACOAs have to make a conscious decision to love ourselves. It is something we have to learn how to do because we haven't had the experience of loving anyone. If that doesn't make sense to you, if you're going to protest that you have spent your life loving your alcoholic parent, think again. Was it genuine love you gave to your parent? Or was it a suicidal devotion just like your parent's self-destructive devotion to herself?

When you were growing up, your alcoholic parent

couldn't teach you how to love because she didn't know how. She knew only how to play the game of manipulation: *If you do this, I will do that.* In her case it was: *If you will help me to continue destroying myself, I will love you.* It wasn't genuine love she was offering, but you didn't realize it. Neither did your parent. You developed the habit of playing the alcoholic's game because you were involved in it from the moment you were born. You grew up in a vacuum of self-deception and self-loathing where the honesty of real love couldn't exist. You accepted the substitute for the real thing because that was all you and those close to you knew. And you responded to the manipulation in the only way you could: You did whatever was asked of you, thinking that was the way people loved, and you hoped that in return you would be loved. Your parent asked for your sacrificial devotion, and you gave it. Then you watched in horror as your parent kept on deteriorating.

You blamed yourself when your alcoholic parent refused to allow you to rescue her. You concluded that your devotion wasn't good enough, your sacrifice wasn't great enough. You would do better the next time. And there always was a next time. Eventually you became conditioned to playing the alcoholic's game, and you called it love. But genuine love does not demand the sacrifice of the self. Nor will it destroy the self. It is passionately interested in the loved one's well-being and safety, but refuses to take responsibility for them. And it is just as passionately interested in the well-being and safety of the self.

How could you really care about your alcoholic parent's well-being and safety when you didn't care about your own? Where did you learn how to care? From a parent who wasn't able to care? Impossible. Did you ask for nothing in return for all you gave? Or were you willing to do anything, even destroy yourself, to get your parent's approval? Did you encourage your parent to grow? Or did you assume responsibility for her? Did you try to protect her from harm by facing the truth about her alcoholic condition? Or did you deny it because you felt helpless to do anything about it?

If this destructive behavior is endangering your welfare and requires buying into your parent's game, then it isn't love. If you want to learn what the real thing is like, let your adult teach you. Don't wait. Your need is urgent. Your best safeguard against self-destructive behavior—your own or anyone else's—is your own ability to love yourself. If you love yourself, you're going to protect yourself.

"As you grow emotionally and spiritually, you will automatically attract people to you who are also growing in those ways," says Vincent DiPascuale. "You'll share who you are with others, but you won't sacrifice yourself any more. When you learn how to love yourself, you become aware that your own self is unique and special, and it belongs only to you."

DiPascuale has a personal credo for constructive living:

> "I accept responsibility for my own decisions. I can grow with them.
> "I start to trust other people. I allow them to get close to me.
> "I realize I don't need a lot of people. I allow special people to get close to me.
> "I allow myself my humanness. I allow myself mistakes.
> "I stop putting so much pressure on myself. I don't have to be perfect.
> "I'm just me, today. What is, is."

Enjoying What We Do

On the day I graduated from college, I took one quick look at my degree, rolled it up again, then gave it to my mother. It was not a gift, but a gesture of anger and defiance. I should have been proud to graduate because I had worked very hard to do it, but I wasn't, because my mother took the credit for it. For four years she had fought my determination to get through college, and sometimes I thought seriously about dropping out. But I kept myself going by telling myself, "Just one more semester." When it became obvious that I was going to get my degree, my mother's attitude changed. Suddenly, my going to college was *her* idea. It was *she* who encouraged me to finish.

I shouldn't have been surprised. It had happened before, and it was to happen again. Whenever I accomplished something, my mother seemed to take it away from me. I was especially frustrated as a writer. Whatever I wrote—from my school-day essays to my first published book—my mother tried to rewrite. I didn't have enough self-confidence to know whether she was right or wrong, but if I didn't agree with her, I felt so guilty that I made the changes anyway.

After a while I stopped showing my mother any of my work, but that didn't help. I could always imagine what she would say about it, and that robbed me of my own objectivity. Finally I wasn't able to finish what I started because I became so self-critical. For a long time I stopped writing at all.

Roy knows how I felt. "I didn't work for almost a year," he says. "I stayed home and lived off my parents. It drove my father nuts, but it gave me a perverse kind of satisfaction. It was as if I was saying, 'Here, you want what I am? Well, I'm nothing, and you're welcome to it!'

"Finally one day I realized that I was hurting myself more than my father. I was living like a bum. I didn't shave, I lived in pajamas, I was out of shape. I didn't talk, I didn't think. I had no money of my own. That's no way to live!"

Roy was beginning to see that his life had fallen into a pattern. To please his father he strove for success, but when he was successful he worried that his father would take away his achievement. "He could do that so easily," he said. "All he had to do was look at me and say, 'I taught you everything you know, and I hope you remember that.' In a way that was a warning to me. He was telling me, 'Don't go too far—I'm the big cheese around here.' And I took that to mean that I'd better trash my success if I wanted to hold on to my old man. I got to the point where I didn't work at all. It was the only way I could avoid competing with him and get back at him at the same time. I wasn't thinking of myself then. I was thinking of him."

Roy now finds that it's important for him to enjoy what he does for a living. "I don't chase success anymore. If I do something well, I take pleasure in the doing of it, but I'm not looking for prizes that I can lay at my old man's feet. When you like what you do, the satisfaction belongs to you, and that's something you're not willing to give away—not to anyone."

Like Roy, I can enjoy my work as a writer now. But I had to become my own person before that could happen. I had to claim ownership of my own abilities. I had to accept personal responsibility for my work, whether it succeeds or fails. I couldn't blame my mother or anyone else for interfering or for appropriating, because I'm perfectly capable of protecting myself from such things. And I did. I simply ignored my mother's suggestions because I didn't feel obligated to please her. I *was* obligated to please myself. When I did, my

mother stopped reading what I wrote. That hurt. It
would have crushed the child in me, but I let my adult
deal with it. She knew I would recover, and she was
right.

Success and failure are still important to me now,
but for different, more practical reasons. I'm not afraid
of failure. I don't seek it, but I know I can survive it
and learn something from it. I want a reasonable
measure of success because it makes it possible for me
to live the kind of life I enjoy and to do the kind of
work that's important to me. But I'm also interested
in getting personal satisfaction out of what I do. Sometimes, just to be sure I have my priorities where they
ought to be, I ask myself these questions:

Am I doing work that gives me satisfaction?
Will I enjoy the doing of it even if it doesn't turn out
    to be successful?
Does doing my work well make me feel successful,
    or do I need recognition, reward, and praise to
    make me feel I've achieved something?
Do I enjoy recognition, reward, and praise? Do they
    enable me to go on to more challenging work?
Will a greater challenge give me more satisfaction?
    If it doesn't, do I feel free to pass it up?

How to Take a Risk

Recovering from self-destructive behavior doesn't mean
that we can't take risks. Loving ourselves should make
it possible for us to take the right kind of chances—
healthy ones that offer us opportunities to gain what
we want without losing more than we can afford. But
remember that risks aren't for children. If you rush
headlong into dangerous situations, or if you're just

the opposite and can't make a move even when you're threatened with disaster, then you're letting your child take on responsibilities she can't handle. Find something age-appropriate for her to do while your adult evaluates your chances and makes your decisions.

It's important for ACOAs to accept a risk as a normal part of life, rather than as a suicidal demonstration of devotion or something to be avoided at all costs. Many of us think of risks in terms of major events, such as financial investments, aggressive career moves, or relocations—challenges that only the daring take on. We overlook the fact that we encounter risks every day. For instance, we take risks when we enter into a relationship, or when we gain an insight into ourselves, or when we respond to people in new ways, or when we set our own goals and pay attention to our own needs. We're breaking old patterns of behavior and we don't know what kind of responses we might provoke. If we rush into risks without regard for our own well-being, we may damage ourselves beyond repair, but if we avoid them, we may miss out on the growth and maturity that life offers us. Spontaneity is the name of this game, and no guarantees are offered. Self-sufficiency means that we're willing to take our chances: We may not always get what we want, but we know we'll survive.

A few years ago I had the opportunity to work on a project that was very important to me, but I almost walked away from it because the woman in charge of it reminded me of my alcoholic mother. She was intelligent, excruciatingly dependent, and manipulative. Within five minutes of meeting her I felt guilty, selfish, and every inch the responsible child. When I learned that the woman was a recovering alcoholic, I thought, "That's it! I'm leaving!" Fortunately I didn't say it out loud.

Everything else about the rest of that day went

badly for me. I didn't trust my footing on escalators. I wasn't able to express my thoughts concisely. On my way home I drove as if every other driver was out to get me. I was depressed about life itself. At long last I realized that I wasn't behaving like an adult. Out of an old habit, my child had begun playing the alcoholic's game, even though the recovering alcoholic hadn't—yet.

As I began to function as an adult again, I considered what the project itself offered me. I needed research experience, and the subject matter was fascinating. The woman in charge was a talented scientist who needed an experienced writer. If we could work together, both of us would benefit from it professionally. Personally, it was an opportunity for my adult to demonstrate, most convincingly, that she could protect my child from abuse. In every way, the situation was risky, but I decided to stay on. I thought I could gain more than I might lose—and if I didn't, I knew how to take care of any wounds I might get.

Almost immediately, I sensed trouble. The woman in charge of the project almost overwhelmed me with praise that I knew I hadn't had a chance to earn. Then she began to give me more and more of her authority, while at the same time describing some personal problems she couldn't seem to solve. But I saw what was happening. I felt my inner alarm go off and I respected it. I knew that my child was safe and that I could take good care of her. I knew, too, that I didn't have to hurt anyone in order to defend myself. I kept in mind my reasons for taking part in the project, and I made sure that I got what I wanted out of it. I cut short meetings that turned out to be unnecessary. I found something else to do when conversations turned to personal problems. By acting on behalf of my own interests, I was able to resist the temptation to take responsibility for someone else's life. But an unexpected benefit was that the recovering alcoholic apparently saw that she, too, was regressing by trying to play the alcoholic's game—and she stopped. We didn't become friends, but we ended our working relationship as respected colleagues.

An ACOA has to consider risks from the vantage point of "What's in it for me?"—and sometimes we have to do our calculations within fractions of seconds. It helps to construct some guidelines ahead of time.

Before you take a risk, protect yourself by asking these questions:

- Am I trying to do or get something I want? Or is it what I think someone else wants?
- Will it enhance my life?
- How much of myself will I have to invest in this risk?
- Can I afford the investment?
- Can I afford to lose my investment?
- Can I survive losing it?
- How long will it take me to recover from losing it?
- What will I lose if I don't take this risk? (This is the most important question to ask if you're afraid to take any risk at all. Don't forget that doing nothing or repeating the same self-destructive behavior can be dangerous.)

If you love yourself, if you really care about your own well-being, you'll know from your answers whether or not to go ahead.

CHAPTER TWELVE

OUR SPIRITUAL SELVES

YOU'LL NOTICE, as you make contact with other ACOAs in recovery programs, that many of them talk about "a higher power." They attribute much, sometimes all, of their progress to a higher power's influence. Some believe that they have been helped by direct divine intervention and care. The Twelve Steps that are the core of so many new and established recovery programs are based upon the acceptance of a higher power.

In Alcoholics Anonymous, that higher power is God—a Christian God at that. Although Step 3 refers to "God as we understand Him," and could be interpreted as an ecumenical description, AA meetings traditionally end with a recitation of the Lord's Prayer, straight out of the New Testament. In a few instances, when the presence of nonbelievers is acknowledged, the prayer is omitted, but these are considered special circumstances. Many of AA's recovering alcoholics and members of their families speak unhesitatingly of Jesus Christ and of being reborn as Christians as a result of accepting and practicing The Twelve Steps.

Some of the other recovery programs take their cues from AA, and although they don't actually promote Christianity itself, they assume a Christian God in their versions of The Twelve Steps. A few other programs define a higher power as God, but refer to him in terms that are more mystical than religious.

"When I use the word *spirituality*," Vincent DiPascuale

tells his audience, "please, please, please, please, please, PLEASE! don't think *religion*.

"Spirituality means how you visualize yourself as a person. A spiritually handicapped person is someone who does not like who he is. He always puts himself down. Sometimes he uses his problems to avoid dealing with the healthy individual inside of him. He wants to avoid growing up. He wants to make other people take care of him. But a spiritually healthy person is mature. He has a lot of self-esteem."

"Spiritual awakening is crucial to the ACOA's recovery," says Loretta Sandy, interim director of Breakthrough. "But I don't mean religion or belonging to a church. I mean something much broader, such as an understanding of where an individual fits into the universe, and how our lives are interrelated, and the meaning of life and death. This is the part of the person that suffers the most damage from the effects of alcoholism. But once a person begins to recover spiritually, the other areas of his life heal more quickly."

Dr. Jean Kirkpatrick of Women for Sobriety is comfortable with the Unity approach to spirituality. "I think it's a good idea to spend at least twenty minutes in meditation at the beginning of each day. I believe that we are what we think, and although I can't stand the phrase, 'We write our own scripts,' I agree with it. I can't accept this idea that the only way to recovery is to turn ourselves over to God—that only reinforces our feelings of helplessness and dependency. I think *we* have to make the changes in our lives by using what God has already given us."

"When I began going to Al-Anon, I was very serious about turning myself over to God," says Elizabeth. "It was hard for me to do that because I always had to control everything, but I thought the change would do me good. So I stopped worrying, I stopped trying to fix things, because I expected God to take care of everything.

"Well, after a while I began to realize that nothing was happening in my life. My problems were getting worse, and all the things I wanted to do weren't working out. Then I talked to a friend of mine and she said I had it all wrong. 'Of course, you're supposed to do something about your life,' she said. 'You *should* make plans and work on your problems—but then you should turn the *results* over to God.' So that's what I do now. I do the best I can with my life and I trust God to make things work out right. And if they don't, I try to come up with some more ideas and go at it again."

"My spiritual life is very important to me," says Dr. Yvonne Kaye. "I don't mean religion, because I haven't practiced religion for many years. But I mean an awareness of God. I learned about unconditional love from God, because, considering my background and my own addictions, there was no way for me to love such a person as myself. But *he* could and he does—and *I* do now."

There are very few Jewish ACOAs in these programs, and many Jewish alcoholics and their families say they avoid them because they aren't comfortable with a Christian orientation, however subtly it may be presented. A relatively new organization known as JACS (Jewish Alcoholics, Chemically Dependent Persons and Significant Others) has its own version of a Twelve Step program. "More and more Jews are struggling with addiction—that's the discouraging part," says Barbara Abrams, assistant executive director of Jewish Family and Children's Service. "But the encouraging part is that the Jewish community has had its consciousness raised. We're not denying the problem anymore." Her organization now offers workshops for addicts, alcoholics, and their families.

Our Inner Selves

Although my religious background is Christian, I am uncomfortable with the heavy emphasis AA puts upon a Christian faith. I have known ACOAs to recover without such a faith and with no definable faith at all. Yet always they have made contact with some kind of inner power, and I think that is conducive to recovery. So when I use the word *spiritual* in this book, I am referring to my conviction that there is more to each human being than our physical, mental, and emotional capacities. Not all of us call it by the same name. Some ACOAs call it a spiritual power, some a higher power, some Buddha, some a life force, some Jehovah, some Christ, some man, some Mohammed, some God, some humanity, and some just say "it." Whatever we call it, we became aware of our power as we were recovering from our alcoholic families. Many of us believe that our recovery wouldn't have been possible without the energy and continuing encouragement that power provided.

You could say that we believe there is such a thing as love—genuine love. We believe it because we have been changed by it. No one ever proved to us that it exists. We can't see it or touch it or hear it. But we know it exists because we *are* loved—for the first time in our lives.

In my case I grew up knowing the name of God. My mother talked about him often, and because she had talked about him since I was an infant, I assumed that such a person existed—more or less. My stepfather assured me that he did. I was afraid of him, this punitive, angry, mean, conniving God of my mother's life. Afraid that if I didn't say my prayers at night he would strike me dead before morning. Or make me get sick. Or make something terrible happen.

Finally, when I was very miserable one time in my early teens, I refused to pray at night. I think I really wanted God to strike me dead because I was so unhappy to be alive. I had just attempted to kill myself by swallowing a box of Midols, which was the only medication I could find in the house. Naturally nothing happened, but when my mother came into my room and found me lying on my bed, face up with my hands folded on my chest, she was furious with me. She was mean-drunk, which was why I wanted to kill myself; I couldn't take it anymore. She accused me of pretending to be sick, of being dramatic and looking for sympathy. I couldn't help it—I blurted out that I had taken the Midols to kill myself. In a typical adolescent passion I hoped that at last my mother would realize how much she had hurt me—but too late.

"Sorry, dear," my mother said sarcastically, "but you'll have to go on living. Aspirins would have done a better job." Then she staggered out of the room.

Later that night when I went to bed I could hear my mother and stepfather arguing in the living room, and I decided I would not pray again. Ever. It was as close as I dared to come to saying that there was no God. The truth is, I didn't want there to be a God like the one I heard about from my parents. I was daring him to prove to me that he was real by snuffing out my life—and he didn't. So, he wasn't there after all, I decided. Actually I felt a little lost. Even a mean God is better than no one at all.

Then I went looking for him. Over the years I attended different churches, learning just enough about some denominations to mumble along in the services. And at one time I really threw myself into religion by working with some church committees. That was when I was married to my first husband, who came from a

family of practicing atheists. I wanted to rescue him—
naturally. That's what an ACOA does, isn't it? I did
rescue him, and he became such a believer that he
tried to do some rescuing of his own. When his mother,
an atheist, died, we buried her with all the trappings
of a Christian funeral, much to the distaste of her
relatives.

God, to me at that time, was like a CEO, and it was
my job to fit into his organization. Eventually I didn't—
but then I didn't ever fit well into groups, so that was
no surprise. For the next several years, God and I
coexisted. I didn't bother him and he didn't bother me.

It was only after I managed to make a complete
ruin of my life and all my relationships that I decided
to put God to another test. This time I didn't dare him
to kill me. I just dared him to love me, because it
seemed that no one else did. After all, what could I
lose? There wasn't a single human being I knew who
could help me, so why not ask God? My life was out of
control, thanks to my enormous efforts to control it.
God couldn't do any worse. As for my proof of a higher
power, I had plenty of it. Alcoholism was a higher power
in my life. Abuse and lack of love were higher powers.
I couldn't see those things, either, but I sure knew
they existed. It didn't take much more to believe that
there really might be a God.

This time I didn't fancy him in any particular way. I
didn't care what he was or how he was because, you
see, I didn't have anybody. Or anything. I wasn't choosy.
I couldn't even call him by name. "Help" was all I
could say. But saying it did something for me. It was
an infinitesimal amount of genuine love I was offering
to myself—in that I deserved to be treated kindly. It
was the first time I had ever offered myself love.

I think that was the beginning of my awareness
that there really is a higher power in all of us. I call it
the inner person. Some people call it the soul or a

higher consciousness. Whatever we may call it, we can't see it or prove it, but we know it is there. We feel it. And in the better moments of our lives, we express it.

Being Spiritually Alive

During all the years while I was a child pretending to be an adult, I had no time to look inward. I was too busy trying to find out what other people expected of me. It never occurred to me that I already had an identity, but if it had, I probably would have assumed it wasn't any good, because I didn't think *I* was any good. I never asked, "What makes me what I am?" because I didn't like what I was. I was trying to be someone different, someone who could be loved.

When I stopped pretending to be an adult and allowed my real adult to look after me, love became part of my life. I thought it came from somewhere outside of me, because I hadn't felt loved before. Actually it was in me all along, except that I wasn't aware of it. I was looking for something quite different. I thought love was something tangible, like someone taking care of me, but that is the way we express love, not what love is. Love is being alive, being human, being like other people yet different, being one incredibly tiny, magnificent particle in an incredibly vast, magnificent creation. Love is what enables my adult to take care of my child. It also enables me, as a whole person, to take care of others. This is what I discovered in myself when I called out, "Help." It was part of my being, but I had never made it part of my life, so it was very new to me. Love is my inner person, the real me, my spirituality. It is what someone who loves me, loves.

I see the inner person in each of us as our individuality, our character, our sensitivity. It has a language of its own that needs no words—it *knows* what is meant. It has its own special way of looking at the world and pays no attention to the latest expert analysis. It sees what matters and cares deeply about such things. It is no pushover—this is where our courage and determination come from. It isn't good or bad, right or wrong, wonderful or ordinary. It is our self, the person we would like to be if only we could. And we can.

Don't ask me what the inner person looks like; we can't see it. Besides, it's different in each of us. But we know it's there. At times it is more real than the face we see in the mirror, or the hands that rub each other warm in the cold. This is our genuine, unique personality. And if our recovery goes far enough, if we stop trying to become what others expect us to be and become what we are, then this inner person and the person we show to the world will become one and the same.

CHAPTER THIRTEEN

GETTING THE HELP
WE NEED

IT'S VERY HARD for ACOAs to ask for help because it makes us feel like failures. "Even today, asking for help in solving problems is often considered weak," says Breakthrough's Kathleen Diak. "The ACOA usually feels disloyal to her parent when she goes into a recovery program. It's a built-in reaction developed over a lifetime, so it's hard to change. We try to make the point that getting help is really a sign of strength."

Getting help makes sense because ACOAs have to start from scratch to find out what some people learn much earlier: who we are and what we can expect to get out of life. We don't know those things because no one was there to teach us, but we certainly have the capacity to learn. We have to learn how to tick—and discover what made our ticking mechanism go wrong. We have to learn how to repair the damage and live productively. None of it will be easy. Or fast. Recovery takes a lot of *very* hard work, and a long, long time. But, as any recovering ACOA will tell you, life gets better all along the way.

Recovery Is Everywhere

Help isn't hard to find. In fact, it's everywhere. The difficulty is in finding the right kind of help, the kind that enables us to change our lives, the kind that lasts.

Today there are so many children of alcohol- and drug-addicted parents that recovery has become a big business. So big, in fact, that recovery programs are now offered not only to children of addicted parents but to anyone who grew up in a "dysfunctional" family. When you consider that "dysfunctional" is used to describe a family in which members can't relate to each other in a healthy manner, you're referring to a large portion of the civilized world. Add to those numbers the amount of attention finally being given to their problems and you will understand why new forms of recovery are popping up everywhere. Is there anyone who doesn't need help?

Yes—to a degree. Many people grow up without severe emotional handicaps. And even among those of us with disabling problems, not everyone needs the same kind of help or the same amount or for the same length of time. And the most valuable effort each of us can make is to help ourselves.

Before you go into any recovery program, look into the kinds of treatment that are available. Choose what you believe suits your particular needs. Give it a chance to work, but if you discover that you made a mistake, don't be afraid to get out and try something else. And be prepared to work. No recovery program can help you unless you're willing to help yourself by practicing what you learn.

Therapy of all kinds has had some bad press, much of it from those who are threatened by the changes it enables people to make in their behavior and their relationships. Also, there are plenty of incompetent therapists, just as there are incompetents in any other area, and they are the ones who attract attention. But no matter how good the therapist—or the program—he or she can only guide you to an understanding of yourself. You are the one who has to use what you learn to turn your life around.

Recovery programs for ACOAs differ according to the type of counseling they offer, the fees they charge, and the amount of time the program requires:

Counseling

In self-help groups such as those sponsored by Adult Children of Alcoholics, AA's Al-Anon, and many lesser-known organizations, there are no professional counselors. Self-help means exactly what it says: the members help each other and function as support groups. They counsel each other, drawing upon what they have learned from their experience with similar problems. Breakthrough's Kathleen Diak says that some self-help groups have such a thorough understanding of ACOA problems that "they can almost be considered professional."

Self-help groups often serve as auxiliaries to professional forms of therapy. It's not unusual for their members to be in private therapy and facilitated programs as well as the groups.

In facilitated programs, such as those in Caron Counseling Services, trained professional counselors work with ACOAs in groups and also in one-on-one sessions. The meetings are educational in nature; they are intended to make ACOAs aware of their problems, to help them to understand their origin, and to point out the possibilities for recovery. They serve as an introduction to therapy and encourage participants to seek further treatment with professional counselors and self-help groups. Many civic, religious, and community health organizations offer facilitated programs.

In private therapy, ACOAs work individually with a psychiatrist, psychologist, social worker, or other professional counselor. The aim here is to help the

ACOA remove the obstacles to personal growth and make contact with the emotions.

Cost

Most self-help groups are free, although a basket may be passed at meetings.

The fees for facilitated groups range from a few dollars per outpatient meeting, to a thousand dollars for an inpatient program, and several thousand dollars for an extensive inpatient program.

Private therapy fees range from fifty dollars an hour to one hundred and fifty dollars, depending upon geographical location and the prestige and training of the therapist. Contact your local community health organization for information about fees in your area.

Note: Some, but not all, of these costs are covered or reimbursed by some medical and health insurance policies.

Time

Self-help groups are open-ended. There is no beginning—you just walk in—and sometimes no end. Al-Anon's ACOA groups, like those in AA for alcoholics, consider membership to be a lifelong participation. Meetings usually are held once a week, for an hour or an hour and a half.

Facilitated courses last for a specified amount of time, anywhere from several days or weeks of concentrated, inpatient treatment to weekly meetings for a number of weeks. There is a definite beginning and end to these programs, but upon completion members are often advised to seek subsequent forms of therapy in self-help groups and private counseling.

The length of time required for private therapy depends upon the needs of the patient and the methods of the therapist. Treatment can range from a few weeks to several years. Parallel participation in self-help groups and facilitated programs is often advised.

A Few Notes of Caution

When I looked into some of the recovery programs available to ACOAs, I was surprised to find that in a few very important ways they may work against recovery. While I don't believe this is intentional or a matter of carelessness, I think it may have something to do with an incomplete understanding of the ACOA— and, something far more subtle, the influence of alcoholic-related theory in ACOA programs.

The negatives, as I observed them, are that many recovery programs:

- Reinforce dependency instead of promoting self-sufficiency
- Do not recognize a difference between the treatment needs of women and men
- Perpetuate the game-playing between alcoholics and the children of alcoholics

Reinforcing dependency

Marian has been attending Al-Anon meetings for eleven years. Recently, at the urging of her Al-Anon sponsor, she began attending ACOA meetings, but she still goes to Al-Anon. The meetings take up two evenings out of her week. She is considering going to an ACOA meeting in another community one night a week. She is the first to arrive and the last to leave. As she walks into the meeting room and sinks into a chair, there is a smile of relief on her face. "Ah-h-h!" she sighs. "I didn't think I'd make it!" She says the same thing every week. During the hour-and-a-half meeting she is animated. She listens intently to each speaker and usually responds with compassion and concern. She is a favorite with the group and the one most often asked to lead a meeting when no one else volunteers. When the hour and a half is over, anxiety returns to her face, and as the next-to-the-last person says good-bye, Marian walks slowly out to her car in the lighted parking lot behind the church.

Paul is an unofficial greeter of new members at an Al-Anon-sponsored ACOA group. He is warm, dynamic, and always ready to poke fun at himself. "What do you expect?" he'll say after he describes a failed attempt to communicate his feelings to his wife. "I'm an ACOA!"

Paul drops in on several groups throughout his area, and he can tell you which ones are the best—the best being those whose members keep coming back. He gets upset when people leave the group, and sometimes he'll call them up and try to talk them into returning. The way he sees it, if you leave the group, you're going to fall back into your old habits. The only way to recover is to stay in the group. If you ask him, "For how long?" he'll shrug and say, "For good—what else?" Then he'll give you a flyer describing an ACOA regional conference and ask you to sign up. "You'll have a great time!" he'll tell you. "You'll meet some wonderful people." Or, if you can't make that, how about an ACOA dance later in the week? If he knows you better, he might even ask you to join him on Saturday when he's going to help an ACOA friend move. Or to come along when he picks up an ACOA group member at the airport.

Paul's a good guy. He does a lot of things for other ACOAs, but he doesn't have much time for anything else. He says his wife complains about that all the time. "But I don't want to stop coming here," he says. "I need you."

Ellen got a lot of help from her meetings. "It felt good to be with people who understood what I was up against," she says. "But I wanted to go on from there. I didn't want to be an alcoholic's daughter all my life. I don't want to define myself that way. When I stopped going to the meetings, some of the members called me up to ask if everything was all right. And when I said yes, everything was fine, I could tell they didn't believe me."

The purpose of self-help groups is to allow people with similar problems to share their experiences and encourage each other to solve their problems. Unfortunately, when no professional counselor is present, the group can easily get caught up in its own emotional conflicts. Instead of making progress toward solving problems, it can perpetuate them. For instance, when several dependent people get together regularly, they are likely to behave in a dependent manner—which is more comfortable because it's an old habit. They'll tell each other they're making progress, yet they'll spend most of their time reliving the past because it's more familiar to them. They usually don't realize that they're digging themselves deeper into their ACOA behavior because there is no objective, professional counselor present to call their attention to it. Even more seductive is the feeling of commonality they have with each other: It gives them a false sense of success in their efforts to build healthy relationships; it makes them less willing to experience the discomfort of behaving in new, independent ways; and it discourages them from interacting with non-ACOAs, which would give them opportunities to evaluate their progress in personal growth more realistically.

After attending a self-help ACOA group for several

weeks, I began to notice that each one of us was behaving like a frightened child pretending to be the parent of another member. When one woman described her dependent relationship with a friend, I immediately went to her rescue with all kinds of advice about how to break it off. Fine, you may say, isn't it wonderful that I was giving the woman the benefit of my experience? But, that isn't what I was doing. I was trying to solve her problem and make her happy. And I did *not* feel wonderful about it! Inside, I felt the same old panic I used to feel when my mother was unhappy. Undoubtedly, I could have been helped if someone else realized what I was doing and pointed it out to me. But no one did, because all the other members of the group were doing the same thing. You never heard so many solutions to one problem.

When I began to realize what was happening, I talked about it. And did I ever feel like a partypooper! The rest of the group began behaving like wrong little kids and I felt guilty for spoiling their evening.

This is not an unusual occurrence in self-help groups. In fact, I interviewed many recovering ACOAs who had dropped out of self-help groups, and their reason was almost always the same: Instead of being dependent upon the alcoholic parent, they became dependent upon the group—and the group considered it progress.

In facilitated groups, the same behavior tendencies occur, but an objective professional counselor is present to call attention to them. By "catching themselves in the act," the group can then begin to identify their dependent behavior patterns, become aware of them in their other relationships, and make important changes.

The needs of women and men

"Don't forget that Alcoholics Anonymous was founded by two male alcoholics," says Dr. Jean Kirkpatrick.

"For many years women weren't even a part of AA because it was assumed that alcoholism was a man's problem. We know now that it isn't, and wasn't. But men are still in charge of most of the recovery programs for alcoholics and their families, and most of the programs are based on those of AA, which are male-oriented. The needs of women are different from the needs of men, and this is not being addressed in most programs.

"In our culture women grow up with a lot of guilt and dependency, and the problems of alcoholism only add to it. They feel *much* more helpless and unworthy than men do, and their need for self-esteem and self-confidence is more urgent." Dr. Kirkpatrick believes that AA's Twelve Step philosophy reinforces feelings of powerlessness, "and women already have too much of that."

"You have to consider that the standards for many recovery programs have been set by AA, and their deficiencies also show up in other groups," agrees Karen Schulte, M.S.W., who specializes in alcoholism and related problems. "But AA was started a long time ago, when our society's needs were quite different—certainly less sophisticated. Now we're beginning to realize that different people have different needs, and today's more sophisticated people may have needs that AA doesn't meet. One of the more outstanding needs today is for more gender-directed programs. But, when it was started, AA was intended for white males.

"It's harder for women to find their way into recovery programs—often because the programs aren't sensitive to their distinctive needs. Even the way the chairs are arranged makes a difference. If they're in rows, one after another, that's indicative of a male-oriented atmosphere. It's very rough on a woman to get up in front of all those linear seats and relate experiences that are very painful. We feel too vulnerable. Being safe is more important to us than it is to men because men's defenses are better developed by our culture. Women are more relational; we're more comfortable sitting in a circle. I think all recovery programs have to begin approaching women's needs differently, especially in the initial stages of treatment."

Dr. Yvonne Kaye has found that self-help groups make much faster progress toward recovery when they work in separate groups for men and women. "Some groups decide to split up on their own," she says, "because they realize that they don't approach their problems in the same way. I can understand that—I can manipulate a man quite easily because he doesn't think the way I do, but a woman can see right through me every time."

Most recovery programs, however, do not yet offer gender-appropriate forms of treatment, although some are aware of the need for it in specific situations.

At Caron Counseling Services there is no attempt to separate the groups according to sex, except for groups of couples. "When it comes to discharging anger," explains Mary Hoffman, "it's sometimes better for both the man and the woman if the partner isn't present. But other than that, we see no reason to separate men from women in our programs. It's true that sometimes the women begin to defer to the men, probably out of cultural habit, but the counselors spot it right away and bring the matter up for discussion in the group. We think that's helpful."

In Starting Point's treatment program, men and women begin by meeting separately and then meet jointly later. "Many women ACOAs need to talk about incest and physical abuse, which are often present in alcoholic families, and it's much harder for them to do that when there are men present," says Vincent DiPascuale.

Breakthrough does not separate their groups. But

they have noticed a higher percentage of women than men in their programs. "Men come here for specific problems—they may have marital troubles or career hangups," says Kathleen Diak. "They start out with something like that, and in the process they get to know more about themselves as human beings. But women seem to be more aware of their emotional difficulties, probably because they're more in touch with their feelings. And women demonstrate more willingness to deal with their problems."

In the programs I observed, it was apparent to me that women quickly deferred to men in the group. They usually waited until a man brought up a subject for discussion before they spoke. If something was troubling them, they often waited until a meeting ended and then took someone—usually another woman —aside to discuss it. Although women are becoming more aware of their need to assert themselves, I didn't notice this awareness in the ACOA meetings I attended. And as long as so many groups fall back upon dependent roles, I see little opportunity for the women in the groups to gain the self-confidence that is so necessary to their recovery.

The alcoholic's game

Many ACOAs become alcoholics, and in recovery programs no distinction is made between them and ACOAs who are not alcoholics. This is unfortunate, because their problems and needs are not the same. There also is a lot of hostile tension between them. Put them together in even the best of programs and they will attempt to play the alcoholic's game. If a counselor can make them aware of what they are doing, something valuable may come out of the experience, but if a group is on its own, the game will take them captive.

"It's a mistake to put them together," says Yvonne Kaye. "Alcoholics—even if *they* were children of alcoholics—want no part of ACOAs. They don't even want to hear about them because it reminds them of so many things they don't want to face."

In the beginning of recovery, the ACOA needs an environment free from the influence of the alcoholic. It is hard enough for her to stop playing the game, but it's almost impossible for her to do it with several games going on around her. Later, when she is strengthened by the nurturing relationship of her child and her adult, she can begin to deal with the alcoholics in her life. But if she has to take on such a burden in the beginning, she may never get that far.

As Dr. Geraldine DePaula explains, "An alcoholic ACOA who's going to ACOA meetings is at the very, very beginning of a very long road. But a sober ACOA is halfway along. It's not that they're on dissimilar roads, but they're in different places along the journey. And the difference is not appreciated. They both have a lot of work to do, but the one who's maintaining the substance abuse is much more into denial and much more into maintaining an unconscious state."

Selecting Your Own Recovery Program

No recovery program is perfect, but that shouldn't prevent you from getting the help you need. It's out there, and if you inform yourself about the pros and cons of various kinds of treatment, you can use what is best for you and avoid the rest. Most recovery programs state their goals quite specifically, and they don't try to accomplish everything. Usually, however, we who need help expect one-stop shopping—and recovery doesn't work that way. We have to get help from several sources.

I have to admit that I favor private therapy, partly because it helped me but also because I have known many other ACOAs who have benefited from it. There is something to be said for working on your own with a skilled professional toward the discovery of yourself. To the outsider it may seem like an ego trip, but I found it to be very hard work that yielded exciting rewards. It's almost impossible to deny, avoid confrontation with the past, and put off making changes when there is only you and a person who wants you to become you. While the fees may hurt, they can also spur you on.

For very good reasons, many psychiatrists recommend that their ACOA patients also participate in self-help groups and facilitated recovery programs. Private therapy is a very special world and you can get lost in it. Working with other ACOAs accomplishes some things you can't get on your own:

- The realization that other people have problems like yours
- The proof that recovery is possible
- The opportunity to experience your individuality within a group

The best kind of recovery for you is the one you select yourself. Use each type, but take only what you need from it. Don't be afraid to make mistakes. You can correct them. Your child isn't running your life anymore—you have an adult in charge.

Self-help programs are useful in several different ways. They are an especially good way for an ACOA to begin recovery because they're casual, inexpensive, and on-going rather than structured as a program. And when you're among other people who can speak openly about their alcoholic parents, you'll find it easier to consider your own shame, hurt, and anger. The camaraderie in self-help groups can be encouraging—as long as you don't begin to transfer your dependency to them. If you find yourself living for the night of your next meeting, it may be time for you to skip it. If the group seems to be dwelling on the same old aches and pains every week, it's definitely time to get out. Don't ask for the group's approval—*you* make the decision.

Facilitated programs are excellent ways to approach recovery, as long as you accept them as that and not as treatment in themselves. They will tell you what is going on inside you and what you can do about it, but they won't *get* inside you. These programs will inform your mind about your problems, and in the beginning that may be all you can handle, but they can't get near your emotions.

Finding sources of treatment isn't difficult. Self-help groups such as Al-Anon and Adult Children of Alcoholics are listed in the telephone book; there are probably chapters near you. If none is available, these organizations will give you guidelines for forming your own support group. If you seek a facilitated group, call your local hospital or community health organization for information. Teaching hospitals, medical schools, community health organizations, and professional organizations can refer you to therapists in private practice in your area.

A very important point for you to remember throughout your recovery is that you are not a label. You may be able to identify with every single one of the ACOA characteristics, but that's not all you are. You're a person, and there is so much of you waiting to be discovered. That's what recovery is all about.

CHAPTER FOURTEEN

MAKING POSITIVE USE OF NEGATIVES

WHEN ELIZABETH was released from a mental hospital twelve years ago, she was pronounced recovered from her breakdown. But there seemed to be nothing left of her past to salvage for a future. Her husband was remarried and had custody of their three children; Elizabeth didn't even have visitation rights. Her mother was divorced from her alcoholic father and was struggling with her own problems. Elizabeth was trained as a nurse, but she had worked at it only briefly during the early years of her marriage.

"I couldn't face the bleakness," she says. For the first time in her life she began to drink heavily and ended up in a twenty-eight-day detoxification program. "I started to feel much better there because I was eating properly and not drinking, but I considered myself an alcoholic and that scared me. I began going to AA and a therapist because I didn't want to be like my father.

"My therapist didn't agree that I was an alcoholic. He thought I was trying too hard to solve all my problems at once. 'Take one step at a time,' he told me." Elizabeth decided that the first step was to bring her training up to date, so she went back to nursing school. Then she got a job in a hospital and rented a small apartment. "I had a bed and very little else, but it was mine," she says.

Her most important goal was to see her children again and, if possible, to build some kind of relationship with them. "They were so small when I had my breakdown, and I was a stranger to them. Later I found out that my former husband never told them I was sick or that *he* divorced *me*. They thought I just went away and left them.

"I gave up nursing because it didn't pay well, and I got a job in medical sales. I was able to furnish my apartment and save some money, but when I asked my former husband and his wife if I could see the children, they told me to stay out of their lives. I asked them over and over to let me visit them for a few hours a week—or even once a month. They said no. 'You're only hurting them by doing this,' they told me. 'They don't want anything to do with you.'

"I don't know why I persisted, but I did. I was proving to myself that I could earn a good living, and I was making friends. I bought a small house so my children could feel at home when they visited me. I didn't want to take them away from the home they knew and loved, but I wanted to have some place in their lives."

Elizabeth was attending Al-Anon meetings and some of the members in the group suggested that she consult a lawyer to determine whether she had any legal rights to her children. "I got the name of a lawyer from a friend. When he heard my story, he said, 'I can't believe this is happening,' and agreed to take my case. He knew I couldn't pay a lot of money and he charged me very little, but he was so helpful. We were in and out of court for two years, and all that time my former husband and his wife kept telling me I was a monster because I was ruining my children's lives. My lawyer said it was very important for me to keep calm and not lose my temper with them, because that would have hurt my case. So even when their lawyer kept trying to portray me as unstable and ready to go back into a mental hospital, I had to keep my cool. I did. I kept reminding myself what the case was all about—that I wanted to see my children.

"We won. I was awarded visitation rights one weekend each month. Then came the hardest part: getting to know my children and waiting for them to want to know me. It took a long time for that to happen, because they were very resentful at first. They wouldn't call me 'Mother' because they called their stepmother 'Mother,' and that hurt. Then I learned that they thought I had abandoned them. When I told them what really happened, they didn't believe me at first. So I had to wait again, until they knew me well enough to realize I was telling the truth.

"That was a hard time for all of us, but it showed me how far I had come. If ever I wanted approval, it was from my children, but I wasn't going to sacrifice myself for it. I knew it would hurt if I never got it, but I also knew I'd survive."

Elizabeth's children are grown now, and their relationship with her is close and loving. "We're good friends, which is more than I ever believed would be possible. I'm 'Mother' now."

Looking back on those years, Elizabeth thinks that the strength to persevere came out of her long experience with frustration. "I had to put up with so much neglect while I was growing up, I guess it gave me a high tolerance for frustration. It's not something I'd want to do again, but during the two years I went from courtroom to courtroom, proving I was a fit and competent mother, I was able to use that same tolerance for frustration to help myself. It's what kept me patient and calm when it was absolutely essential for me to be that way. But now, when I use something from the past, I don't do it for nothing. I make sure I get something out of it for myself."

Finding Value in the Past

As painful as our past may be, and important as it is to free ourselves from it, it's not a good idea to erase it entirely. We can still use some of the behavior we learned there, but in productive, positive ways.

"ACOAs are survivors," Yvonne Kaye points out. "The fact that we're here, alive, functioning, breathing —that's something to be proud of. Now we've got to learn how to live. We've got to look at the tools we used to survive—some of which were denying, manipulating, withdrawal, overreacting, control—and ask ourselves, 'What's positive in any of these things? How can I use them to help myself?'

"Think about this matter of control, for instance. If we're in business, then we'd better know how to use control properly. Controlling the actions of other people in business is *direction*. That's what a boss or a supervisor does, and it's a valuable asset. But we have to learn when and how to use it.

"I used to have trouble with authority. I didn't like to take orders from anyone. But now I find that I'm very good at working on my own. Being responsible for myself doesn't overwhelm me, and I don't need a lot of people around me. I don't feel isolated when I'm alone—I can get my work done. And that suits my needs very well. I can also stand up and speak to an audience of a thousand people; that's making positive use of that same quality that resisted authority."

When I was in college and living at home, I had a heavy course load, but it was very hard for me to study. Either there was too much commotion going on when my parents were drinking, or I was constantly alert for signs of trouble. Gradually I developed an ability to tune out whatever was going on around me and concentrate on my work. I could hear things but not be caught up in them. Unfortunately, I also tuned out my emotions because that was the only way I could ignore my anxiety, and they stayed tuned out.

Years later, when I began to get in touch with my suppressed emotions, I exulted in my freedom to express them. But one day when I was very upset about something and also had to do some research I couldn't put off, I began to wish I could simply tune out my distress. Then I thought, *Why not?* By that time I had distinguished my child from my adult, and I realized that my discomfort was coming from my anxious child. That consciousness put me into my adult mode where I was able to calm my child by telling her I would take care of our problems as soon as I finished my work— and then we would go for a nice long walk. Almost immediately my tension began to ease and I was able to concentrate on what I wanted to do. I didn't tune out my emotions; I asked them to be quiet for a little while. I knew they deserved respect and had to be dealt with, but at a more convenient time. And when I was ready to deal with them, there they were, waiting for me.

I'm also a very patient person. I can put off gratification for a long time. Without a doubt, these qualities were developed or strengthened by all the broken promises that alcoholic parents typically make to their children. For many years of my life I could put off gratification because I really didn't expect anything. But now that I do expect to get something good out of life—in fact, it's one of my goals—I find it useful to be able to wait for my efforts to bear fruit. As a writer, I find patience absolutely indispensable; getting thoughts out of my head and onto paper takes time.

If you are at that point in your recovery where you are becoming aware of your negative behavior patterns, don't outlaw them. You may be able to rehabilitate them by considering these possibilities:

- Is the behavior negative because your child is taking on something he can't handle and not doing it well?
- Are there any worthwhile qualities in the behavior?
- Can your adult make some positive use of those qualities?

If you can turn your negatives over to your adult, you may be able to salvage something valuable from your past. And whenever you can do that, you're healing some of your hurt. Even the memories of past events associated with these patterns of behavior will be far less painful for you to recall.

Loving Ways

The most satisfying part of recovery for adult children of alcoholics is the discovery that love is freedom, not bondage. It is a respect for others that grows out of respect for the self.

Any one of us can tell some pretty dismal stories about our efforts to save a parent from alcoholism. For many years of my life that was my all-consuming goal. But now I don't feel compelled to rescue someone who doesn't want to be rescued. Nor do I waste my time trying to help someone who isn't willing to help herself.

When I began to realize how much of my sympathies had been lavished on people who ridiculed them, I vowed never to hold out my hand again. I thought my mistake was to love. But it wasn't. Caring about someone in distress is, in itself, something of value. It's part of my spiritual self, something I wouldn't want to be without. It isn't what I *am* that did me in, but how I *used* what I am. Now I'm learning how to care without becoming a patsy. I'm making progress by letting my adult administer my caring.

In many similar ways ACOAs can use, *in our own behalf*, some of the same responses that once bound us to loveless relationships. Our loyalty, when it is offered to those who deserve it, is a vital part of friendship and intimacy. Our seriousness reminds us how important our recovery is, especially when the going gets rough. Our imagination, once used to cover up the nightmare of our lives, and even to lie, can be used to visualize a better future.

"Last month my daughter and I went to a father-daughter dinner at our church," Martin recalls with a big smile. "I'll tell you, I almost cried, it was so beautiful. I was so proud, dancing with my daughter. I've always tried to be a good father, and being at that dinner was like proof that I was.

"I hated being my father's father, but this is different. This feels natural."

Sara believes that one reason she enjoys teaching is that she cherishes the child in her. "Maybe I missed part of my regular childhood," she says, "but I make up for it in other ways. I enjoy teaching small children, and I spend as much time down on the floor as they do. We have a lot of fun—fun is part of learning, don't you think?

"I can't count how many times I've seen *Snow White and the Seven Dwarfs*—and any other Disney cartoon. When a new one comes out, my husband knows I'll want to see it. He doesn't even ask, we just go. My children make fun of me, but I don't care. I have a great time."

Doug enjoys coaching a teenage swimming team in his spare time. "Kids that age need something to do," he says. "But I get as much out of it as they do."

Elizabeth has gone back into nursing. "My children are on their own now, and I don't see them as often," she says. "I don't need to make as much money anymore, and I have a small nest egg. I can afford to do something that gives me more satisfaction in a deeper sense." Elizabeth works in a hospice for terminally ill cancer patients. "I sought this out," she says. "I don't find it morbid at all. In a way, I've had to face a kind of death many times, and I'm not afraid of it anymore. I really want to help some other people reach that point." She seems to be a happy person.

Caring for others, at the same time we care for ourselves, is part of our recovery. It's not unusual to find recovering ACOAs working in areas where they can perform valuable human services. Sometimes it is their main occupation, sometimes they volunteer. Either way, their expressions of love are bringing them satisfaction rather than frustration and pain. Perhaps they are putting into practice what many ACOAs said to me when I asked to interview them: "I'd love to be able to help someone else break free." When I began to realize that I was a loving human being, and not the unfeeling creature my parents found it convenient to label me, I felt the same way. Perhaps I knew all along, in some remote part of myself, that I was forbidden to love rather than incapable of it. The removal of that taboo was pure freedom.

Beyond Recovery

The literature about ACOAs deals mainly with recovery from our trauma. But we are more than accident victims, and there ought to be more to our future than overcoming the past. This is one of the reasons why I disagree with the attitude that the child of an alcoholic parent is going to be that for the rest of his or her life. As popular and as helpful as the ACOA label may be in identifying what went wrong with our lives, we should reach a point where we no longer need it. We should reach a point where recovery is behind us, and life itself is our primary preoccupation.

This is why I hope that, before too long, the current forms of treatment will begin to go beyond identifying our problems and warning us of worse ones to come. However well-intentioned many of these programs may be, they can't heal us by transferring our love needs from someone destructive to someone or something benevolent. We need to learn how to love ourselves in the reciprocal, responsible, enjoyable way that adults and children normally love each other. And then we can move on. Recovery, no matter how effective it is, is not the same as living a life, and living is the business of human beings.

If you are the adult child of an alcoholic parent, then I urge you to make use of every form of recovery available to you. But use them as *you* see fit. Don't get stuck in any one of them. Make it your goal to grow beyond recovery. Once you have given yourself the childhood you never had, and when you allow your adult to look after you, you'll be fine.

I can't think of a better way to summarize what lies ahead of you than these lines which I found, framed, in—of all places!—my dentist's waiting room:

A CHILD LEARNS WHAT HE LIVES

If a child lives with criticism, he learns to condemn.
If a child lives with hostility, he learns to fight.
If a child lives with ridicule, he learns to be shy.

If a child lives with shame, he learns to feel guilty.
If a child lives with tolerance, he learns to be patient.
If a child lives with encouragement, he learns confidence.
If a child lives with praise, he learns to appreciate.
If a child lives with fairness, he learns justice.
If a child lives with security, he learns to have faith.
If a child lives with approval, he learns to like himself.
If a child lives with acceptance and friendship, he learns to find love in the world.

—DOROTHY LAW NOLTE

ADDITIONAL READINGS

Berne, Eric, M.D. *Games People Play,* New York: Ballantine Books, 1964.

Black, Claudia. *It Will Never Happen to Me,* Denver, Colorado: M.A.C., Printing and Publications Division, 1982.

Beattie, Melody. *Codependent No More: How to Stop Controlling Others and Start Caring for Yourself,* New York: Harper & Row, Publishers, Inc., 1987.

Brandon, Nathaniel. *Honoring the Self: Personal Integrity and the Heroic Potentials of Human Nature,* Boston: Houghton Mifflin Company, 1984.

Christopher, James. *How to Stay Sober: Recovery Without Religion,* Buffalo, NY: Prometheus Books, 1988.

Dowling, Colette. *The Cinderella Complex: Women's Hidden Fear of Independence,* New York: Pocket Books, 1981.

Erikson, Erik H. *Identity: Youth and Crisis,* New York: W. W. Norton, 1968.

Fromm, Erich. *The Art of Loving,* New York: Harper & Row, Publishers, Inc., 1956.

Kirkpatrick, Jean, Ph.D. *Goodbye Hangovers, Hello Life: Self-Help for Women,* New York: Ballantine Books, 1987.

Koller, Alice. *An Unknown Woman,* New York: Bantam Books, 1983.

Langer, Ellen J., *Mindfulness* (Addison-Wesley, 1989, $16.95)

Norwood, Robin. *Women Who Love Too Much,* New York: Jeremy P. Tarcher, Inc./St. Martin's Press, Inc., 1985.

Peele, Stanton & Brodsky, Archie, *Love and Addiction* (Signet, 1987, $4.50)

Peele, Stanton, *Diseasing of America: Addiction Treatment Out of Control* (Lexington Books, 1989, $19.95)

Powell, John S. *Why Am I Afraid to Tell You Who I Am?,* Allen, TX: Argus Communications, 1969.

Rodegast, Pat, and Judith Stanton, compilers. *Emmanuel's Book, A Manual for Living Comfortably in the Cosmos,* New York: Some Friends of Emmanuel, 1985.

Rubin, Theodore, with Eleanor Rubin. *Compassion and Self-Hate: An Alternative to Despair,* New York: David McKay Company, 1975.

Smith, Ann W. *Grandchildren of Alcoholics,* Pompano Beach, FL: Health Communications, Inc., 1988.

Steiner, Claude, Ph.D. *Games Alcoholics Play,* New York: Ballantine Books, 1971.

Vaillant, George E. *The Natural History of Alcoholism: Causes, Patterns and Paths to Recovery,* Cambridge, MA: Harvard University Press, 1982.

Viorst, Judith. *Necessary Losses: The Loves, Illusions, Dependencies and Impossible Expectations That All of Us Have to Give Up in Order to Grow,* New York: Ballantine Books, 1987.

Woititz, Janet Geringer, Ed.D. *Adult Children of Alcoholics,* Pompano Beach, FL: Health Communications, Inc., 1983.

HELPFUL RESOURCES

For literature and general information:

Al-Anon Family Group Headquarters
P.O. Box 862
Midtown Station
New York, NY 10018-0862

National Association for Children of Alcoholics
31706 Coast Highway, Suite 201
South Laguna, CA 92677

Children of Alcoholics Foundation
200 Park Avenue, 31st Floor
New York, NY 10166

Health Communications, Inc.
1721 Blount Road
Pompano Beach, FL 33069

National Clearinghouse for Alcohol Information
P.O. Box 2345
Rockville, Maryland 20852

National Council on Alcoholism
12 West 21st Street, 7th Floor
New York, NY 10010

National Institute on Alcohol Abuse and Alcoholism
5600 Fishers Lane
Rockville, Maryland 20857

For information about local resources:

Call the local chapter of the above organizations. You'll find their current numbers listed in your telephone book.

Call your local hospital or community health group for referrals to self-help groups, facilitated groups, resident and nonresident treatment programs, and private therapists.